BOVEY
AN ANCIENT TOWN

Its Story and Legend

Lance Tregoning

Cottage Publishing

First published in Great Britain in 1983
This edition with additional material from the author published 1993
© Minola Tregoning 1993

Published by
Cottage Publishing
72 Fore Street
Bovey Tracey
Newton Abbot
Devon TQ13 9AE
Tel: (0626) 835757
Fax: (0626) 835758

British Library Cataloguing in Publication Data
CIP Catalogue Record for this book is available from the British Library
ISBN 1 897785 02 X

Designed, typeset and edited by
Nick Harman
Cottage Publishing
Tel: (0626) 835757

Printed by
Moor Print, Manaton, Devon

Front cover photograph: Bovey Bridge and Riverside Mill.
Rear cover photographs: 19th century view from Bovey Bridge west along Station
Road together with the same view today; and the author Lance Tregoning

CONTENTS

DEDICATION

To the memory of the late Lance Tregoning who died on 1st July 1991. This revised edition has been made possible by the kind assistance of his widow, Minola Tregoning.

J.L. Tregoning was born in 1917 in Bovey Tracey and lived there all his life. On leaving school he worked for about 15 years at his father's grocer's shop at 72 Fore Street. During world war two he served in the Devonshire Regiment. He was then a company representative before working in the offices of a local company Wyatt and Bruce. He was churchwarden for twenty eight years and had access to many of the records formerly kept in the church.

The new approach steps to the south door of the parish church were dedicated to Lance Tregoning in 1992. A plaque to this effect is mounted on an adjacent wall.

He was known to many as a keen local historian. He wrote two books; the first publication of Bovey Tracey an Ancient Town, was self published in 1983, and Bovey Tracey in Bygone Days was published by Devon Books in 1989.

ACKNOWLEDGEMENTS

History is what it implies, and cannot be changed. Many of the things described in this book have already been written about before. I have endeavoured, by further research, to embellish them where possible, and add many other items which have come to light; while the last one hundred years are covered by actual recollections of people alive at the time, from whom, over the years, I have gathered and recorded their accounts of life as it was.

I gratefully acknowledge the help given by:

The works of William Ellis
The unpublished work 'Bovey Beads' by the Rev'd Barry Hyde
'Sketches', by Mrs M. A. Hole
Material from Lt. Col. E. R. Jones
Rev'd G. O. C. Duxbury, M. A
Elizabeth Prince
Armitage Hargreaves
Mrs Mary Pruen
Molly Bent
Les Manley
also the recollections of many inhabitants of the town, past and present, too many to mention by name.

The publishers wish to thank the County Local Studies Librararian of Devon County Council for the kind assistance given and for permission to reproduce the maps dated between 1765, 1827 and 1887.

Illustrations for the legends by Brenda Gilpin.

FOREWORD

This is the history of a town and its people – it is not an historian's account as such, but the story of a place and its people, (with its historical sources where possible) from its earliest beginnings up to the present.

Many of the earlier memories and legends are from word of mouth, handed down from father to son in succeeding generations. Many contain items of fact which can be placed even in the present day; some are vouched for in official writings and histories, some even in the equivalent of Hansard.

Many of the stories were first written down for posterity by a former inhabitant of the town William Ellis, in the mid nineteenth century. He emigrated to America, but returning again in his latter years. His writings were effusively victorian, but contained all the facts needed. Where he gave dates, he was remarkably accurate.

The later stages from the 1920's onwards are mainly recollections of myself and my friends. I have for most of my life been a lover of history, particularly the people of that history. I can stand in an old place, our church for instance, imagine the countless numbers that have gone before and be at one with them in spirit, as in any old place that has a past.

So, I hope I can take many of my readers into the past with me, show them how their forbears lived, and give an idea of the growth of our community. I hope that this will strengthen the ties of our present town and help to carry it forward into the future in a way that will be admired by our successors.

1

THE EARLIEST BEGINNINGS

It now seems that organised life and settlements in our area go back in time further than many have thought. Research has brought to light some evidence of one of these settlements.

It was at Plumley the name is of saxon origin and means 'a clearing in the plum trees'. (Beara is also saxon, meaning a grove of trees).

Up to 1836 at Plumley, there were six hut circles in one of the large fields. In that year, excavations were commenced and eight bronze axeheads were found together with smaller items such as beads. Three of these axeheads were sent to Exeter.

The ones at Exeter, now in the archaeological section of the Royal Albert Memorial Museum, have been classified and carbon dated by the experts as Bronze Age, approximately 1000 B.C. So we know that there was an organised settlement in Bovey, at least 3000 years ago. Unfortunately, the circles have now disappeared, as have the other five axeheads.

Through the centuries, handed down by word of mouth, there has been the legend of a Roman granite built villa or rest camp, sited somewhere around the present site of Lancehurst in Challabrook Road. Until the end of the last century it was known by the name of Vagabonds Stoneborough. This is shown on some survey maps up to the middle of the last century. The 19th century name comes from the practice of wandering gypsies using it as a camp.

This was noted by the Reverend Barry Hyde in his research into Bovey history, and while no positive proof can be found it seems that up until the middle of the 19th century the stone ruins of a building could still be found. This, if correct, would date Roman activity to around the year 300 AD.

In a book published in 1851 by Dr Frazer Halle and Dr John Croker (of Cross Cottage) there is a description of a find on Knighton Heath, just prior to that date, of two Celtic moulds, spindle or canoe shaped, enamelled and engraved on light blue serpentine.

They were discovered when digging one of the many small clay pits on the heath and were at a depth of about 6 ft. One mould measured 2 feet (60cm) in length, with a circumference of 10 inches (25cm) and the other was 1 foot 9 inches (28cm) long and 11 inches (31cm) in diameter. According to the authors both were probably used for casting metal spearheads or rapier like blades.

At that time the moulds were in the possession of the proprietor of the pits, Mr Davy of Chudleigh Knighton, but their present whereabouts is not known. These are a further indication of the probability of organised life in this area. Dated around 1300 BC, copies of the moulds can be seen in the Royal Albert Memorial Museum in Exeter.

From samples taken in 1861, it seems that the Bovey basin clay beds are as deep and thick as 500 feet. Fossil plants identified then, include sequoia fir, ferns, palms and custard apples, indicated a warm climate of the Eocene or Miocene period, which may be unique in England. The Bovey basin is recognised by experts as being unmatched in its geological construction.

. At Wooleigh it is known there was mining, probably for tin, but also for the mineral tourmaline, a semi-precious stone which was found here and is a fairly rare occurrence elsewhere. There are no traces of the stones now, but many years ago they must have been quarried in some quantity and probably sent all over the then known world.

Much more recently, a find in Drake Lane (not yet expertly certified) poses the fact of saxon occupation in the area. During excavation for a new bungalow at the conjunction of Drake Lane with Coombe Close, a kist vaen or cist (a burial place) was found, covered by a very large stone. Inside were found pieces of pottery, bones and a gilded saxon saucer brooch made of bronze. Some play has been made that the brooch is of brass, but this is not correct. There are also several small barrows or tumuli, on the opposite side of Drake Lane below the conjunction with Coombe Close and a little further down. These are possibly a product of the bronze age or even earlier.

Another find was at Elsford, during the early 1800's. According to *Crossings Guide to Dartmoor*, a cairn or kist vaen was discovered and excavated, and in it were found a copper spearhead, an amulet of stone and some glass beads.

The antiquity of Little John's Walk may be verified by the fact that it is part of the parish boundary, probably one of the few saxon roads or tracks existing in the area.

2
SAXON TIMES
(400 A.D. - 1066)

The very earliest records of the town appear to be made by the saxons about the years four to five hundred A.D. when there was a small settlement beside the river, in the triangle formed by the tracks which are now Fore Street, Hind Street and Mary Street. There was either a ford or a clapper bridge over the river, which was known to have been used by the Romans.

TRACKWAYS

Tracks from this settlement led away, one up from Mary Street to Atway, where it crossed the track and bridle way from Parke (via Southbrook to Hennock). One track then led on to Moretonhampstead and one up over the hill via Whitstone and Ashwell spring, across Crownley and on to Five Lanes and Hennock. A very ancient cross stood at the crossways at Atway, origin unknown. That same cross can still be seen, now let into the wall at Cross Cottage at the top of Mary Street. A further track led up through what is now East Street, on to Bradley, Wifford and Little Bovey and so to Twin Yeo, where the Teign River joins the Bovey – at which point it was tidal in those days.

The fields on the north side of Wifford were named by the saxons 'Bibbery', or Beavers Lea, from a large colony of beavers found at this point. The great dam formed by these animals made a wide and shallow stretch of water safe for crossing and thus called Wifford or 'Wide Ford'. The tracks in those days followed the course of rivers where possible and one ran by the river to Kingsteignton and Teignmouth and was the route used by the Danes, Vikings and similar pirates on their forays into south Devon. Another track led from Five Lanes and Hennock across to Little John's Walk and on to Lustleigh.

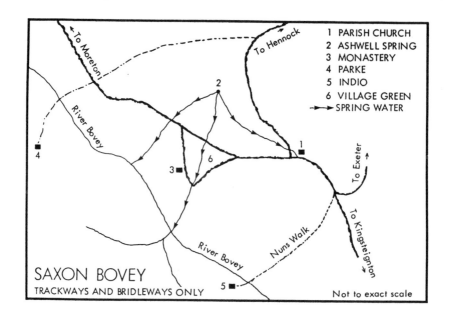

1 PARISH CHURCH
2 ASHWELL SPRING
3 MONASTERY
4 PARKE
5 INDIO
6 VILLAGE GREEN
→ SPRING WATER

SAXON BOVEY
TRACKWAYS AND BRIDLEWAYS ONLY

Not to exact scale

THE SPRINGS

There were, and still are, an abundance of springs in the Bovey area – the main one, the Ashwell Spring, giving rise to many legends. The Ashwell Spring divided, one part running down over Furzeleigh to the bottom of Mary Street, joined by another one at this point, named Bladder Shute (a name which probably came from the custom of villagers using the stream to clean the offal from their slaughtered pigs).

The second part of the Ashwell Spring came down Traw Lane (Trough Lane) to the ancient trough by the parish church. Another source of water was down the hill to around about the village green (where the Town Hall now is). These springs formed the water supply for this end of the town.

The very first church was built at the site of the present church, probably because of the presence of water, about four to five hundred A.D. It was built by a Christian missionary of mud and wattle, who also built his first Oratory here. Every church since has been built on that same site.

LEGEND

Also about this time at the end of the saxon period, the legend of Traw (Trough) Lane spring is set. It seems the sexton of the parish church (then made of wood on the site where the church still stands) was carrying buckets of murky water to his house beside the church, for use during the services. He had hardly set them on the floor, when a knock came at the door and a strange lady of sweet countenance stood there, dripping wet from the storm which raged.

She was at once asked in to share the homely supper. Seeing the sexton's wife was in deep mourning, she asked the reason. On being told that she had that day buried her first and only child she expressed deep sympathy and promised she would have many children and grandchildren in the future.

She then asked for a drink of water, and noticing its foulness she asked if it was for the use of the church. On being told it was, said: 'It is too dirty for holy water, and too foul for the font'.

When ready to leave, she asked the two of them to accompany her a short way. After climbing the first part of Trough Lane she stood for a moment and gazed heavenwards, upon which a cool crystal spring gushed forth of which she said: 'This will continue pure and cool for my church throughout generations'.

This spring was later enclosed with stones and became known as St. Mary's Well. The most golden of frogs lived in it (vouched for by William Ellis, who

St. Mary's Well (probably saxon)

said it was still so at the beginning of the 1800's). The stone trough was hewn and placed in its present position, where a stream still ran until the 1960's. The spring was taken over by the South West Water Company, and the flow of the water has since disappeared.

Unfortunately the springs source itself is now buried and covered over, but still runs, partly down over Trough Lane and partly down by Furzeleigh Lane.

LOCAL NAMES

The River Bovey itself is supposed to get its name from a saxon Theign called Bofa or Boui, and gave name to several hamlets – North Bovey, South Bovey, (later Bovey Tracey), Little Bovey and Bovey Coombe among them.

Many of the local place names are of saxon origin, among them Pullabrook, Bottor, Elsford, Hawkmoor and Hatherleigh, (Polebrook, Brungarstone, Eilausford, Hauocmore, Harley). Woolley is probably a corruption of the Cornish Wheal and saxon Lea, meaning probably some mining of copper or tin by British slave labour under the saxons.

The occupation by the saxons seemed to lead to a steady improvement in village life after a long period of misery and ignorance (the Dark Ages). The saxon method of agriculture can possibly be seen in the long narrow lines of the fields and gardens above Mary Street.

Although the native population were enslaved, the wealth and establishment of religion were not affected; the saxons were professors of the Christian faith and apart from the ravages of the Danes and Vikings, life in the Theigns forming the villages continued at a steady pace until the Norman Conquest. The Theigns probably built defensible forts and farms against the invaders.

STORY OF THE DANES

One of the earliest legends of the town also springs from saxon times. The legend seems to have some basis in fact and concerns sea pirates, Danes or Vikings, who were ravaging the coast about this time (the year 996 or thereabouts). They had ravaged Kingsteignton and came on up to Bovey on the Shrove Tuesday, burnt the timber church, and gathered all the villagers together on the village green. They called together seven of the Theigns, and their followers, and they demanded a preposterous ransom. (A Theign was the headman of a farmsteading in charge of all the serfs or labourers)

On one side of the green were a row of houses, somewhat in the fashion of the butterwalks in Totnes and Dartmouth, with the upper stories projecting over the path (two of the pillars to this still exist, at Indio).

Rain began to fall during this assembly and the leader of the Danes took refuge under the projecting upper floor of one of the houses. In the chamber above were stored a number of large cloam jars full of grain where the housewife (unheard because of the storm) raised the trapdoor and pushed one of the jars down on top of the leader, smashing it and him. The villagers took advantage of the disturbance and fell upon the pirates, killing many and capturing the rest.

The custom of the time with such prisoners was to flay them and nail the skins to the church door, but as the church was burnt down, they were kept as slaves, a merciful release. (At the time of the Domesday survey, there were fifteen Theigns or farmsteadings in the parish of Bovey).

3
AFTER THE
NORMAN CONQUEST

KING HAROLD

Bovey first became historically noteworthy at the time of the Conquest; before then the manor of Bovey belonged to King Harold, who often spent time at his favourite country house at Parke, together with his two sons Goodwin and Edmund.

At the overthrow and death of their father, these two fled to Ireland. Later, hearing the disaffection with the Normans, they gathered a mercenary band of Irish and Devonian soldiers, returned, and ravaged a portion of Devon (the South Hams) and Cornwall. They returned to Widecombe with their booty and then crossed to Ilsington, where lived the saxon Earl Erdulf, whose only daughter was Goodwin's affianced bride.

Within 24 hours they were married, but the Normans simultaneously arrived at Bagtor and dispossessed Erdulf; so after a hurried visit to Bovey, Edmund and Goodwin, together with his bride, fled to Denmark, where they spent the remainder of their days.

It seems that as far back in history as then, Bovey was already in favour with royalty.

THOMAS À 'BECKETT

The manor of Bovey was then attached to the Barony of Barnstaple, and eventually passed to the possession of Sir William de Tracey, who affixed his name to that of Bovey, which ever since has been known as Bovey Tracey. He also became involved with Archbishop Beckett.

Bovey church was probably built in varying stages, the main part not until the 14th century; although William Ellis has a theory that this is not strictly correct. His view is that the church was finished in 1176, and that we only have to look at the arches inside the church to see that they are Norman in origin. The windows are of a later period, which is explained by the fact that in 1327 the building was almost destroyed by fire, but the walls and arches still stood, although blackened. The windows suffered the most.

On being rebuilt, the perpendicular style was adopted for the windows, while the arches show a combination of the two, both the round and slightly pointed style. This would give credence to the legend that the church was built by Sir William de Tracey as penance for the murder of Thomas à 'Beckett in 1170. It was dedicated to St Thomas by the Bishop of Exeter in 1176; its saxon predecessor having already been dedicated to St Peter and St Paul. The known and unbroken list of vicars of the church certainly goes back to the year 1258.

The reason Sir William de Tracey asked to be one of the four knights who murdered Becket, is that he feared his wife had had an affair with the Archbishop. She had been a lady-in-waiting to Princess Margaret, the daughter of the french King, when she was in the custody of Beckett, then Lord Chancellor.

When she married Sir William and was installed as mistress of Bovey manor House, (old Parke), she remained very friendly with Beckett. When Becket paid a visit to the Abbot of Buckfastleigh he was the guest of Lady de Tracey and was given the use of a large room, which ever after, was called the Bishop's Chamber. He occupied this room on several occasions.

After the murder William fled to north Devon when he soon discovered that his wife's interest in the prelate was purely spiritual and nothing more, and he was overcome with remorse.

In order to obtain the Pope's pardon, he offered to use a portion of his great wealth to erect a new church in Bovey, dedicating it to the Martyr. As indeed it was.

THE ANNUAL FAIR

It was the grandson of William, Henry de Tracey, who about 80 years later, asked for a fair for the town. This fair, granted to the town in 1260, was for a duration of three days. Also a weekly market was granted to Henry de Tracey at 'his manor of Bovey, on the Vigil, Feast and Morrow, of the Translation of St Thomas the Martyr' (the translation was the placing of the murdered Saint's bones in the new shrine of Canterbury Cathedral).

The first fair was held on July 6th, 7th, and 8th, 1260. The Charter includes the Grant of Free Warren (hunting) in all the demesne lands of the said manor, under pain of forfeiting ten pounds to the King. The fine of ten pounds (equivalent to £1,500 now) seems very heavy when compared to the salary of the King's Chancellor at that time of 5 shillings (25p) per day, plus three loaves, one wax candle, and twelve candle ends.

Henry was closely connected with another great Devon family, the Courtenays, who became more closely related to Bovey at a much later date.

The vicar of that time, probably Geoffrey of Taunton, contracted a debt
upon the Benefice, for repairs, which has never yet been paid off, and the
vicar still pays the rent thereon (not interest, that was forbidden between
Christians in Medieval times) of about £2 yearly – an unredeemed obligation
of about seven hundred years.

SUCCESSION

After the death of Harold, William the Conqueror gave the manor of Bovey
to Geoffrey de Mowbray, Bishop of Coutances in Normandy, William's
Lieutenant at the Battle of Hastings.

In the Devonshire Doomsday Book we find an entry 'Land of the Bishop
of Coutances in Devonshire'. 'The Bishop has a manor called Bovi (Bovey)
which Eddric held on the day on which King Edward was alive and dead (he
died), and it rendered geld for two hides'. (A hide was an area of land between
sixty and hundred acres.) These lands can be ploughed by ten ploughs (an
important pointer in assessing the worth of the manor) and the whole of the
Bovey manor brought in over fifteen pounds a year; so the parish was fairly
prosperous for those times.

On the death of William, the bishop forfeited his lands, and the next Lord
of the manor was Judhael de Totnes, also a Norman nobleman. He in turn,
forfeited his lands, but twelve years later he was re-instated to the Barony of
Barnstaple, which included the manor of Bovey, and there he resided until
his death.

After this it seems that Bovey reverted to the Crown. Probably it was King
Stephen who bestowed the manor on Henry de Tracey (the Tracey family
taking its name from the Norman village of Traci, near Bayeaux). The Traceys
then held the living of Bovey Tracey until the time of Henry III.

There is another legend connected with the Traceys and Parke, but more
of this later. There is an ancient rhyme *All the de Traceys have wind in their
faces*, supposedly originating from the belief that William tried to go on a
pilgrimage after the murder, but that each time there was a great storm which
blew him back. H.V. Moreton believes, however, that he actually went and
in the end he died in the Holy Land.

INDIO

In the 11th Century there were many religious houses in Bovey as well as the parish church. One was a small priory at Indio, the unusual name being derived from the latin words 'In Deo', implying a house, for, or according to, God.

Indio or In Deo is correctly described in Dugdales massive *Monasticum* as being in south Bovey, but erroneously places it in Cornwall, thus causing some confusion. This confirms its existance as a monastery, (afterwards a priory) at least one thousand years ago, but legend has it that it was in existance one thousand five hundred years ago.

The priory remained so until the time of Henry II, when it became a Nunnery, under the superintendence of a prioress. It was finally dissolved in the reign of Henry VIII; becoming a private residence at the beginning of the reign of Elizabeth I. It was rebuilt by Sir John Stawell in 1660 (Whether this was the present building is not known for sure). He was the first Lord of the Manor to live in the town since the time of the Tracey's.

A path with a double hedge led from the priory to the parish church, for the convenience of the Nuns, with a bridge over the river. Part of this and the path, still exists, but more of this in a further legend of Bovey.

Indio in 18th century.

17

HIND STREET MONASTERY

At Hind Street where the present Baptist chapel stands, stood a monastery, the last structure of which was finally demolished in 1822. All that now remains is the main arch, misleadingly called 'Cromwells Arch', with a portion of the south wall, which was once the entrance to the monastery. The smaller arch at the entrance to the Baptist graveyard, (the date on the arch is the date it was renovated by J. Steer) is also part of the original.

Cromwell's Arch (part of the old monastery) and small arch to Baptist graveyard.

Cromwell's Arch, date not known, showing buildings behind now gone.

The monastery can be reasonably dated to around 1170, of early Norman work. It wasprobably at first dependent on the French priory at Caen, and later transferred in the 13th century to the Hospital of St. John, Bridgewater (the parish church also belonged to the Brethen of St. John from 1250 to 1536).

In 1228, there is confirmation of an ecclesiastical grant by Oliver de Traci of a pension from Bovey Tracey to St. John of Bridgewater. Later in 1319, a Royal Letter and Writ was issued to Bovey for non payment of a rent of 109 shillings and 7 pence, owing to the Order of St. John, Bridgewater. No details are given, but it is assumed that as the Hind Street monastery came under St. John, this is the one concerned. It was once endowed with the manors of Wreyland and Heathfield, but was eventually given over to the priory at Buckfastleigh.

It could be assumed that the Norman chapel described by William Ellis as being in existence until 1832, is more likely to be the building traditionally supposed to have been built by William de Tracey in expiation for the murder of Thomas à 'Beckett.

This building was the one used by the Baptist community until that date. The records of the Baptist Association for June 10th, 1831 say, 'The state of our very ancient place of worship gives us much concern, it is a building of saxon, Popish origin, and still bears some vestiges of the superstition of those remote ages, it has stood many hundred years and it is now necessary to rebuild it.' It was demolished in 1832, and the present Baptist chapel built.

Old inhabitants told the young William Ellis that the original buildings covered an acre, with 12 acres of land around it. He describes the old buildings as follows. 'Square or oblong in shape, facing west to east, smallish, 20 feet by 30 feet, there was a round headed porch and doorway on the south side, with a grotesque figure in the centre, the doorway very much like the door of the Bishopsteignton church but more primitive.' Its round headed, narrow windows proclaimed it to be saxon. There was a small gallery inside supported on pillars, also saxon, and a slightly concave ceiling. The porch had stone seats, with room to seat 3 or 4 on either side. It could be that Ellis was slightly wrong in attributing it to the saxon period, it was possibly Norman.

CHARTER

With the granting of the Charter in 1260, the Borough became an institution of which the Burgesses could be justly proud, with, in the case of the Freeman, a change from copyholders to freeholders, with rights of sale, and succession.

The old instruments of the borough are held in the present council chamber – the staves and town crier's bell, quart and pint measures, and scales with four metal weights, as used to measure bread and ale. These are placed in the custody of the Town Trust.

THE MANORS AND LAND TENURE

The manor of Bovey dates from the Conquest, and was governed by its annual Court Baron, which in early times was associated with a View (or Review) of Frankpledge. This means, in essence, that every Frank (or Free) man had to pledge himself to be under the supervision of someone else, for the purposes of the King's peace.

Families within the manor (each freeman of course being responsible for his own labourers, or serfs) were grouped by tens and at their head was the Tithing Man (an office even older than Frankpledge). The Tithing Man was required to answer to the View of Frankpledge at the Court Baron, for the good behaviour and honest life of his group.

Most of the Freemen on an ancient Devon manor were copyholders, and the creation by the Lord of the Manor of a borough within his manor, meant essentially the changing of the copyholders into freeholders, with rights of sale and free succession, with the forming of a civic government. This was constituted in Bovey at a Court Leet held annually (like the Court Baron) at which the Officers were elected: namely, the portreeve, the surveyors of bread and beer, of the ways (or paths), and the collector of Alnage, (a tax on each ell of woollen serge); together with the scavenger, the town crier and two constables (these being kings officers, associated with the churchwardens).

Our borough at this time included amongst its estates: Stantor, West Bovey, Pludda, Hind Street, Mary Street, Fore Street, the Portreeves' Parks, Mannings and Wises Meadows, Friars Meadow, Bradley Ford and Hores Meadow, but not church Style or Drake Lane.

TRADE AND MARKET

During this period the serge weaving industry was flourishing in the parish, for there is record of a small fulling mill for the dressing of the cloth. This survived until the nineteenth century, as can be seen from tomb stones in both the old parish churchyard and in the old Baptist burial ground, bearing the name of Tapper in both eras.

The weekly market at that time, was the centre of the citizen's week. He took to it what he had to sell, and bought what he needed. The shop was a hut or workshop, where things were made to order; of stocks of goods there were none. If you missed the weekly market you might get what you wanted at the informal Sunday churchyard market.

The bill for a party of seven at a local inn, for 24 hours, gives an indication of the prices of the time, i.e.

Bread	4d.
Meat	5d.
Beer and Wine	$3^1/_4$d.
Soup	$^1/_4$d.
Beds	2d.
Candles	$^1/_4$d.
Fuel	2d.
Fodder	10d.

TOTAL 2s. $2^3/_4$d.   (Equal to $11^1/_2$ new pence)

The beds seem cheap, but were of straw, and full of vermin - perhaps not quite the good old days.

MAYOR'S MONDAY

Round about the 14th century, Mayor's Monday began. It was held on the first Monday after the 3rd of May. This was the beating of the bounds by the Mayor and Burgesses on horseback, after which the Mayor entertained all the freeholders of the borough to a sumptuous dinner.

Revenue for the dinner came from an endowment by one of the Tracey family, with a gift of two fields, called the Portreeves Parks'. This ended about 1860 – the fields were sold, the money invested, and this income is now controlled by the Town Trust, and put to much more prosaic uses.

In an account of the ceremony in the mid 1860's, it says the town was garlanded at various points. The Mayor's and Bailiff's houses had triumphal arches and the Union Hotel, where the banquet was held, displayed a profusion of flags and evergreens.

When the event first started the Mayor would ride his horse up to the cross, (whether the town cross, or the cross in Mary Street, is not recorded), and strike it with his stick, (*Omerods Archaeology of Ancient Dartmoor*), thus proclaiming his authority and giving almost the force of a municipal law. Young men would kiss the stone to pledge allegiance in upholding rights and privaleges.

Only one other similar ceremony is known in the whole of Britain, and this took place at the London Stone near Billingsgate.

THE VILLAGE GREEN

The town Cross is generally agreed to have been erected in the centre of the village green by Matilda de Tracey, daughter of Henri, to commemorate the granting of a fair and market in 1260. It stayed there until it was moved to its present position to allow for the building of the Town Hall in the nineteenth century (1864) (See page 57).

Also on the green was a heavy stone with a ring attached for tethering the bull during the horrific sport of bull baiting, which was abolished by law in 1835. This stone has now disappeared.

PLAGUE

During the fourteenth century the plague swept the countryside, including Bovey, decimating the inhabitants including the vicars, as can be seen from the official records. These show that between 1309 and 1401 there were 12 incumbents, the shortest incumbency being 10 days.

The state of the churches must have been disheartening to the bishops at that time. The Archdeacon's report for the parish church of 1342 reads: 'The surplice is worn out, the wedding veil is lost, the paschal council is lost, the statue of the patron saint is badly painted. The roof of the nave is in bad condition and the parishoners are warned that these defects must be put in order before the next visitation, on penalty of one mark.'

In the letter of 30th October, 1348, to all his churches in the Diocese of Exeter, Bishop Grandisson wrote, ordering solemn public processions in the parishes every Wednesday and Friday, also psalms, masses and prayers as these were the proper weapons to combat the plague. The correct reason, fleas from rats, was not even suspected.

THE CHURCH OF ST. PETER, ST PAUL & ST. THOMAS OF CANTERBURY

Bovey church was probably constructed in the late 12th century. The tower is 13th century. The main aisles were burnt down in 1327 (a widely held legend) and then rebuilt.

The Nave and Chancel were largely rebuilt during the fifteenth century, and probably occupied many years in building. Presumably the money came from the parishioners, particularly from the Lords of the six or seven Bovey manors.

The white stone of the pillars came from Beer, to the east of the County, while the granite for the walls and windows is local, from Dartmoor.

The south chancel priests' door which can be seen from the outside of the church beside the Forbes' tomb is considered by the experts to be part of the original 13th century building. The 13th century porch probably had a priest room over it in its original form. The porch boss, of four heads, of 14th century origin consists of the following, Henry II, the Pope, Archbishop Beckett and de Tracey.

In those days the nave of the church was used for many purposes. It was the common parish hall, and the school for the children, as well as an eating place for the congregation after services.

The unbroken lists of vicars dates from 1258, when Geoffrey de Tauntone was presented to the Living by the Brothers of St. John of Bridgewater. He was given the tithes and advowson of the parish by the bishop, with the approval of Henry de Tracey. Geoffrey in 1260 contracted a debt, to rebuild the vicarage. The interest of which, about £2, is still paid annually

JEWES BRIDGE

Jewes Bridge over the River Bovey on the old A38, near the confluence of the Bovey and the Teign, was probably Roman in its original form. When the present bridge was built in 1815 to replace the one then standing, foundations of two previous bridges were found underneath. The name is presumed to come from the name of one of the early builders, Jewe.

It is on record that on 9 December 1421, the then Bishop of Exeter, Bishop Lacy granted indulgencies (i.e forgiveness of sins, granting of prayers) to anyone who would contribute to the repair of Jewes Bridge, then in great disrepair.

4

TUDOR AND STUART AGE

bout this time 14 boroughs were included in the Rate made for the County. Bovey was one of these, rated at two pounds, equal to Tiverton and higher than Okehampton. Plymouth was thirty four pounds.

CHURCH

Until Tudor times, there were no fixed seats, only mats and rushes, and people stood and knelt. In some churches can be found stone seats running around the walls, where weaker members retired during services. This was probably the origin of the saying: 'The weakest go to the wall'.

The end of the fifteenth century was a great time for the furnishings of churches, and the beauty of the decorations in the parish church is undoubtedly due to the fact that the lady of the manor at this time was Lady Margaret Beaufort, countess of Richmond and mother of King Henry VII. She was in possession of the manor throughout her son's reign and the beautiful chancel screen, (reputedly one of the best in the west country), the pulpit, lectern and font were all added during this time.

The paintings of Saints and Apostles, at the base of the screen, are still in the original medieval paint and were not touched when the screen was restored later, and so are almost six hundred years old.

Lady Margaret also built the College, two rows of old thatched cottages which stood below the church, one row of which was demolished in 1896 to make way for the Courtenay memorial, the others standing until the 1950's [See photo page 60]. The present row of houses still bear the old name.

These buildings were founded as a college for clerks, who were officials having the duty of serving at Mass, carrying holy water to all who had paid for it and providing music and singing in the rood loft (over the screen).

The Amorial Bearings of Lady Margaret Beaufort are included in the east window of the church.

Lady Margaret Beaufort

In 1490 the Church House was built at the foot of the stone steps. (This seems to be the earliest record of the building of a house, still standing). This was used for the more secular purposes, which until now the church itself had been used, such as the brewing of cider and ale, (sold for the benefit of the church) and the eating of meals, etc. There was also a Pound at the rear of the house (where the car park no is) for the pounding of apples. In Queen Mary's time, the house was sold, for financial reasons, so unfortunately lost to the church.

According to Cecil Torr, in his *Small Talk at Wreyland*, the strife in the churches over the removal of rood lofts and other ecclesiastical decorations, in the west of England, reached open rebellion in 1549. The rebellion came to Bovey in that year, generally being called 'The Commotion'. Many Bovey folk were involved in this.

In 1577 the loft above the screen was removed and replaced with a gallery at the west end; and about the same time the beautiful old elizabethan chalice was made by Hall of Exeter; this is still owned by the church.

George Manning became vicar of Bovey in the year before the institution of Henry VIII, and it is strongly suggested that he had protestant leanings.

During his incumbency, he helped to destroy the images of the Virgin Mary and St Thomas of Canterbury, also the rood from above the screen.

Further proof is given in the fact that the church bells at Bovey were spared at a time when the bells all over Devon were declared to be forfeit, because they had rung to rally people to rebellion against the new protestant ritual. At any rate, it is interesting to note that it is recorded that in 1553 four bells and one little bell continued in the tower at Bovey church.

When Queen Mary came to the throne, Manning's days were numbered, and in 1554 he was dipossessed and Christopher Petell was made vicar on the presentation of Queen Mary herself. Since that day, every succeeding vicar has been nominated by the Sovereign. This is known as a Crown Living.

Petell brought back the old Latin Mattins and Mass, but when Elizabeth came to the throne, the English Reformation services were revived.

INDUSTRY

Life continued in the town in much the same style as before, with about 1000 inhabitants.

Old documents once kept in the church (now in the Exeter Archives) such as Apprenticeship Indentures, Church House Deeds, Deeds of Trust, Wises Meadow and Mannings Meadow deeds etc. give some idea of the trades of the time. There was a certain amount of weaving and milling industry, but otherwise almost wholly agricultural.

Bovey derived a great deal of its medieval prosperity from wool. There is record of a fulling mill in use in Bovey as early as 1327 and it is known that there were many weaving mills in use in the succeeding years. A fulling mill was still in use in Little Bovey as late as the 18th century. A Mr Moses Savery owned a weaving mill in Bovey in the 1700's. He also owned Bradley, Stonelands, Woolleigh and Eastern Street; a large Landowner.

HOUSES

Many of the houses still standing go back to medieval times. The house now called Manor House in East Street was built around 1200 and may have been the home of the de Tracey's, but this cannot be proven. Some years ago, a secret passage was discovered behind an old fireplace, but this has now been bricked up. The barn next door was also from the same date and especially noted for a fine timber barrelled roof. Most of the framework of the roof was demolished

Front House, also in East Street was built in 1530 and is generally recognised as the source of the Civil War Legend (See chapter 5). Yew Tree House (Rumbling Tum Restaurant) in Fore Street also dates back to the 16th century.

The Old Thatched Inn in Station Road (known also as the Old Dolphin) was the original old coaching house and was built in 1625. It was previously used as an Inn in the 19th century, (in the intervening years in use as a shop).

This is probably the oldest alehouse in the district. (see rear cover, in both photo's to the left of the road.). Pludda Cottage in Station Road, and Atway on the Moreton Road, are of the same period, but there are no known records of actual dates.

Old Parke is generally recognised as the old manor house. It was built around the 12th century and contained the old bishop's Chamber which is believed to be part of the existing outbuildings and has since been used as a grain store.

The late Miss Tracey had in her possession, a Deed, concerning the old house which stood where the Auto Centre was (now Lloyds Chemist). The Deed stated that on 12 September 1577, William Gillbeart, gentleman, son of Edward Gillbeart, sold to Thomas Barkley for £230, his interest in that capital mansion house called 'Henstreate' in Bovie Tracie, Thomas Barkley was to come into possession on the death of Margaret Gilbeart. It has been suggested by some that this could have been the original Manor House.

THE MANOR

At the turn of the 16th century Nicholas Eveleigh lived at Parke, in a castellated building which was probably built by him and which stood until 1827. He was steward of the Devonshire Stannaries and was tragically killed in the performance of his duties at the Stannay Court in Chagford, when the Courthouse collapsed. Nine others were also killed.

About a year later his widow, Alice, married a rich widower named Eliseaus Hele. He was a lawyer of the Inner Temple and treasurer to James I and a very rich man. Milling was one of his assets, for his Will mentions 'All those my Mills in the parish of Bovey Tracey'.

He and his wife are both buried in Exeter Cathedral but placed in the south side of the chancel of Bovey church is an elaborate memorial to them both (also to his first wife and son) showing himself and his two wives and son. On the north side of the chancel is a monument to Alices' first husband, Nicholas Eveleigh, both memorials being erected during her lifetime.

Hele had no children to inherit his wealth, (his son having pre-deceased him) so he left his money to be disposed of in 'Pious uses', from which he became known to posterity as 'Pious uses Hele'.

Among his many benefactions were the Blue Maids School at Exeter (now Maynards) and of course, Hele School. In his will, he mentions a legacy to Blue Maids School of £50 a year from his mills in Bovey. It seems that the School was renamed after Sir Jon Maynard, who held the office of Sergeant to Oliver Cromwell and later King's Sergeant to Charles II.

Sir John died in 1690; as there were twelve girls being educated at the Blue Maids School in 1672 it seems that at least part of the Trust was completed at an early date. In the mid 1600's Sir John Stawell became Lord of the Manor, and lived at Indio thence becoming the first Lord of the Manor to live in the town since the Tracey's. Later in 1658 he became the owner of Parke, to which his son William succeeded. The Stawells had a family vault in the parish church in which most of the family were buried. A slab bearing the Stawell coat of arms lies near the present front pews.

William Stawell presented the silver alms dish to the church which bears his name; this is now on display in the Exeter Museum.

THE VICARAGE

In the last years of Elizabeth's reign, the vicarage was little more than a wreck. An official inventory of that time says: 'Implements of the house there are none, but onlie the bare walls, so that not so much as a forme, bench, windowleaf or glasse of windows is there left, but all taken down and carried away, as also the verie boardes of certain planchings'.

A petition dated 1596 from the parishoners to the Bishop of Exeter referring to rates for maintenance of the church is preserved in Exeter City Library. These kinds of buildings seem to be the only type of which records can be found, and one can only guess that many of the ordinary dwellings were in a similar condition.

PLAGUE

The town suffered badly in many plague years. As it was a market town, it probably spread the plague to many of its neighbouring villages.

The first outbreak of what was known as 'The Black Death' was in 1546-1547. This massive outbreak killed 118 in two years, against the normal of 14 deaths a year. Then in 1551 came 'The Great Sweat', probably a virulent form of influenza. Allied to this in 1555-1556 came two bad harvests, so a combination of influenza and starvation, accounted for another 95 deaths.

Plague again in 1592-1593, was very bad. In twelve months there were 87 deaths. There was terrible human and family suffering. The plague started in April with the Voysey family, there were six deaths, four within two days, and all from one family. Later there were five deaths in the Wetherdon family. Richard Wetherdon lost his wife, two sons, a daughter and a brother; a dreadful toll.

These figures are taken from the parish registers of the time, the earliest going back to 1538 (re-copied on vellum in 1598). They were kept in the church until 1974, when they were then deposited in the Exeter Archives for safety. They still remain the property of the parish, and can be examined by anyone on request.

5
CIVIL WAR

BEFORE BATTLE

In September 1628, Charles I appointed one of his chaplains, James Forbes, to the Living of Bovey. He was an ardent Royalist. It is interesting to note that in 1641, every male person person over the age of eighteen was asked to sign a protestation against all Popery. Of the three hundred and forty five eligible in Bovey, not one refused to sign, including the vicar.

In the name of the civil war, Devon was more inclined to the parliamentary cause, rather than the Royalist, as was Bovey. Both Exeter and Dartmouth were strongly Royalist, and blockaded by the parliamentarians.

At Christmas 1645 there were three regiments of Royalist horse, under the command of Lord Wentworth, camped on the heath between Bovey and Heathfield. (The heath at this time stretched as far as Challabrook). At the same time the parliamentary forces were at Crediton and Moreton, under Oliver Cromwell and General Fairfax.

Cromwell moved from Crediton, capturing Dunsford and Canonteign before Christmas, while Fairfax covered him at Moreton from the Royalists stationed at Okehampton.

Local legend has it that in early January 1646, Cromwell, taking only a few men, advanced to Bovey to reconnoitre. He called at the house of a known sympathiser, named Coniam, living at Lower Atway (where the house stood until about 1890). He left his men there and went on alone down Hind Street to the old monastery, (part of which was used as a presbyterian meeting place) where he learnt of the nearness of Wentworth's forces and of the men actually billeted in Bovey.

After staying the night, he returned to Atway and sent a message to Fairfax to advance at once. He then rejoined his own men to lead them to Bovey. Apparently the prime intention was to capture the newly built bridge over the river (built in 1642).

BATTLE

On the bitterly cold day of January 8th, Cromwell led his men through Hennock and down Furzeleigh Lane and surprised a company of Royalist officers who were drinking and gambling in a house in Fore Street (said to be the Front House).

One of the Royalists had the presence of mind to pick up the stakes and throw them out of the window, and while the Roundheads were scrambling for the money, the officers escaped out of the back of the house, across the river, so getting away.

Local legend seems to favour two houses for this – Front House and the old Riverside House – but Front House seems to fit all known facts. (This is also agreed by the historic buildings society).

On 9 January, the following day, the battle of Bovey Heath was joined, ending in a great victory for the Parliamentarians. The Royalists lost seven colours, including the Royal Standard, 400 horse and many dead; among the prisoners were 4 Colonels, 3 Lieut Colonels, 5 Majors, 11 Captains, 300 arms of various kinds, 140 prisoners and 150 head of cattle. [The site of the battle is marked on the map on page 80]

It has been said that this battle marked the end of the Royalist resistence in the south west. Dartmouth crumbled after this and further resistence was only sketchy.

It was agreed that the Royalist forces were a rabble of unruly layabouts who pillaged the supporters of either side without pity, while they were very poorly led by their officers.

The headquarters, or drums, gave the name to Drumbridges. As recently as 1977, the Civil War Society erected a Commonwealth Cross on the old Breast Works, which can still be seen on the Bovey side of the heath, not far from the caravan park.

LETTERS

The authenticity of the legend of the throwing of the stakes from the window can be vouched for by the writings of Joshua Sprigg, who was chaplain to Fairfax. He kept a detailed account of the campaign and wrote two letters to Members of Parliament, true copies of which have been kept.

The copies are headed as follows: 'A true copy of two letters pertaining to the Civil War in Bovey Tracey. Printed and published by order of the Commons assembled in Parliament, printed by Edward Husband (the equivalent of today's Hansard), printer to the House of Commons, Jan. 15, 1646, and sold at his shop at the sign of the Golden Dragon in Fleet Street, near the Inner Temple'.

'A true relation of the fight at Bovey Tracey between the Parliament Forces under Sir Thomas Fairfax, and three regiments of the King's Horse, wherein was taken four hundred horse and seven colours, with divers officers and soldiers; sent in two letters, one to the Hon. William Lenthal, Speaker to the House of Commons, and the other to the Hon. Edmund Prideaux M.P.'

The letter to the Hon. Edmund Prideaux is the more interesting and runs as follows:- 'To the Hon. Edmund Prideaux Esq. M.P.' Sir. I thought fit to send this expresse unto you, for the better confirmation of that I writ yesterday. We took at Bovey four hundred horse at least, and seven horse Colours, whereof one is the King's, having a crown and C.R. upon it, some officers and soldiers were taken prisoners. We lost but one man, divers of the enemy sore wounded, some slain.

Some of their chief officers being in a house, shut the door and threw out of the window about ten pounds in silver, which the Foot soldiers were so busie about getting their shares, that the officers escaped in the meantime, over the River through the darkness of the night.

About six score of those that escaped got into Ilsington church that night, and sent to the Lord Wentworth for relief.

We drew out a party of horse and foot next morning to surprise them, but they footed it away, and so escaped. The Army advanced next day being Saturday, to Ashburton. Truly our Soldiers march with that cheerfulness as I never seen them before on this service. You shall hear further from, Your Most Humble Servant, Joshua Sprigg, Ashburton, Jan. 11, 1646 at Noon.'

MEMORIAL

A memorial to a slain Royalist officer can be seen on the footpath from Avenue Road to Challabrook. The young man, called Langstone, was killed in the battle, probably on what was then known as Challabrook Heath, although the actual site is unknown.

The rough memorial was erected by the townfolk, because of the young officer's kindness to them, and in the early eighteen hundreds was lost, but was rediscovered by A.J. Wyatt in 1923, serving as a gatepost.

It was erected in its present position, and now bears a metal plate, with the inscription: 'This old cross once marked the grave of a Royalist officer who fell near here in 1645 when Cromwell's troops defeated the Royalists. A.J.W. 1923.'

STOOKES CHARITY

There is another story which can be traced as having a great deal of truth in it, concerning the throwing of the money to the soldiers.

When the stake money was thrown out of the window, one of the officers then playing was said to be one of the Cliffords of Chudleigh. He threw his bag of winnings, (gold coins) to his servant and told him to run, before making good his own escape. The servant jumped from a window, found a horse, and galloped off towards Trusham, hotly pursued by a posse of Roundhead soldiers.

During the pursuit, he threw the bag of gold over the hedge, whether to distract the pursuers, or come back himself at a later date, we do not know. Hiding behind the hedge was one John Stooke, (a farmer's boy, out tending the cattle) who hid, terrified on hearing the clatter of horses hooves. He saw something thrown, and on searching found the bag of coins.

With this treasure he is said to have laid the foundation of his fortune, from which spring's the John Stookes Charity. A document drawn up on 31 May 1709 between Thomas Tothill and John Coniam, states that John Stooke had in his lifetime, given to the father of Thomas Tothill the sum of £100 for the purchase of land; and bought from John Coniam, a tenement and all the lands adjoining, with the wish that the yearly rent of such land should got to the parish church of Bovey Tracey, the rents and profits therein to be used for ever, for the purchase of bread and wine for the celebration of the Holy Eucharist three times a year; three shillings for the vicar, two shillings for any other labour involved, and the residue to the poor of the parish.

The charity still exists, although the land has since been sold, and the money vested in the Charities Official Investment Fund. From this the parish church receives an annual amount for the Altar Fund, usually between £3 and £5.

A memorial to John Stooke and his wife can be seen in Trusham parish church, where the gift to Bovey Tracey is recorded.

JAMES FORBES

The vicar James Forbes, (a scotsman and former army chaplain) was instituted to the living by Charles I. He was deprived of his living by the puritanical Parliament and for eight years had to exist on one fifth of his former income from the Benefice.

Fortunately, the Revd. Forbes was able to secrete the beautiful brass lectern by burying it on the heath and he also hid the church register and the Elizabethan Communion Cup, until his re-instatement.

Being a known Royalist, he was very harshly treated, being harried unmercifully by the soldiery, who frequently despoiled and plundered his house. It is on record that once when £30 was demanded from him, he told them that he would gladly give it if they would buy ropes and hang themselves.

Three incumbents succeeded him in eight years, none of whom was recognised, nor officially recorded in the list of church vicars. The first, called Tucker, was in Forbes' own words 'A most bitter, furious, turbulent fellow' who used to preach with a sword by his side. He tore down with his own hands, the Royal Arms and Commandments and tried to deface the screen, fortunately without much success.

His successor was an even wilder man 'Crackett-brained Christopher Lee'. Life at the vicarage was made unbearable for him by the parishoners who endeavoured to 'make life as uneasie for him as they could', and seem to have succeeded, for he resigned after only a year.

He was replaced by Joseph Edgecumbe, who was a more easy going man, who let part of the vicarage as an ale house and was a friend of the Woolcomber's Club who met there for a drink. He treated Forbes with kindness and understanding which the vicar returned when he received the benefice.

In 1655 at the height of the troubles, Forbes' wife Marion died and was buried, not within the church, as expected in normal times, but outside the south wall of the church.

Her tomb is a large pinnacled rock bearing the Forbes arms and the Rose of England and Thistle of Scotland. It also has a carving of what resembles a mermaid, but is thought probably to represent the Resurrection, in the symbol of Jonah escaping from a large fish.

For the final five years of his vicariate (after the Restoration), the vicar spent his time restoring the damage done by his predecessors, in which he was greatly helped by the then Lord of the Manor, Sir John Stawell.

In 1661 the font was provided with its existing cover, and one can imagine the scene when the lecturn was dug up, cleaned and restored to its rightful place.

LORDS OF THE MANOR

The last Royal Lord of the Manor of Bovey was Charles I. He sold it to Ralph Freeman, Lord Mayor of London, in payment of debts. It was eventually purchased by John Stawell, who, as far as it is known, became the first Lord of the Manor to reside in the parish, since the time of the Conquest. He lived first at Indio, and from 1658 at Parke, eventually being succeeded by his eldest son William. In 1691, William presented to the church the highly embossed silver alms dish, which is on loan to the Museum at Exeter, and can be seen there.

Formerly all our sovereigns were lay rectors of the parish and the reigning Monarch is still its patron. The last vicar to receive the living as a personal gift, was the Hon. Charles Courtenay, who received it from Queen Victoria, as well as being made a Canon of Windsor.

A family vault in the parish church contains the bodies of Sir John Stawell, Lady Jane his wife and his two sons. The vault was built according to his Will in 1667, which reads 'My body to be buried in the Isle of the parish church of Boveytracey aforesaid, which belongs to my house and seate called Indeo, in a vault there to be made where now the great pewe stands'.

The slab bearing the Stawell coat of arms lies near the present front pew and pulpit, while high up on the wall in the south Aisle is a memorial reading: 'Sacred to the memory of Sir John Stawell, Knight Banneret who succumbed to death January 19th 1669 aged 44, also his third son, John who departed hence January 29th 1674, piously placed by William Stawell, only surviving song'.

In 1676 a religious census was taken of the town, which showed a population of one thousand, six hundred and twenty three of whom twenty three were non-conformists, and none were Roman Catholic.

6
THE HOUSE OF HANOVER

RECORDS

For the next hundred or so years parochial records were either not kept at all, or kept and later destroyed, for none survive. However, we do know that the Bovey Grammar School was founded and endowed with Mannings Meadow in 1713-14 (the last year of the reign of Queen Anne), largely through the activities of the Society for the Promotion of Christian Knowledge, and the help of William Stawell.

A schoolmaster was appointed who lived at Yew Tree Cottage, (now known as the Rumbling Tum Restaurant). The school was built where Courtenay House now stands, (now an antique centre and tea rooms).

Indentures dated at this time between one John Coniam and Thomas Tothill, gave the income from Wises Meadow at £6 per annum. This for the salary of the Schoolmaster and all succeeding masters and for the education of seven poor children. He was also allowed to supplement his income by charging moderate fees for not more than ten boarders. He was licensed by the bishop of the Diocese.

CHURCH

About 1700, the then vicar of the parish recorded an inventory of the vicarage of that time. This vicarage stood in what is now the vegetable garden of the old vicarage (Grey Gables) where parts of the old foundations and other artefacts have been dug.

This inventory shows quite a large house – kitchen, hall, parlour, milkhouse and buttery on the ground floor; upstairs were three lodging chambers, a dining room and study; while outside were a barn, a linhay, a brewhouse, stables and sheds. A very comfortable home for those times.

NON-CONFORMISTS

In 1772, the Baptist community came officially into being in Bovey, although there was a meeting place in Pludda. From 1795 to 1843, the Minister was a very popular Parson named Sprague, who lived in a house which stood beside the river, where the water wheel now stands.

He used to baptise his flock in the River Bovey at a spot where the old ducking stool used to be. It is said that the last person in Bovey to be so ducked was a cobbler' wife, who was thereby cured of her scolding tongue. She later joined the Baptist community, (as did her husband) in gratitude, both being immersed in the waters of Bovey. The wife was proud to tell people that it wasn't the first time she had been ducked!

The Parson's house was later occupied by a man named Noah Flood, so it was inevitable that it became known locally as the 'Ark'.

THE DOMMETTS

Back with the parish church again, and on November 1st 1735 began what must surely be a record of sorts: on that date, Philobeth Dommett was inducted vicar of the parish, to be followed in 1786 by his son Joseph. Together they held the office for just short of 100 years.

Tales of them both are legion, and are related by William Ellis; one concerns both Philobeth, Joseph and a Mr Addems, a farmer of Elsford Farm.

Joseph was visited by Addems, who came to pay his tithes. When the vicar consulted his tithe book, he said: 'I can find neither Addems nor Elsford Farm entered here'. Mr Addems said: 'then my father was right', and produced from his pocket a torn sheet from a similar tithe book. Joseph recognised his father's writing, and in astonishment asked for an explanation.

Addems said that, years before his father was in a poor way and was unable to pay his tithe to Philobeth. He had gone to the vicar and had thrown himself on his mercy, explaining that due to illness and a succession of poor harvests, he could not pay. But whatever happened, he would pay them eventually, or his son would for him. Philobeth, knowing the man to be honest, and murmuring something about needing a new tithe book, tore out the page relating to Elsford Farm and gave it to Addems, saying: 'my new book will have no Elsford in it, but keep an account, and one day pay either me or my successor'.

Addems' son then laid £250 and some small change on the table in front of Joseph, saying he would honour the promise made to his dying father. Joseph looked at the young man and said: 'We will divide this in half, which will got to meet your tithes for many years to come, and I will have half, but if ever you are in trouble, as was your father, come to me and I will tear out the page again'. Father and son, both just and generous men.

Both were men of stature, both physically and mentally. Joseph especially was a wrestler of some consequence, as is shown in a report of the time, about

Revd. Joseph Dommett

food riots during the period of the Napoleonic Wars, when prices had risen so much that there was a great deal of suffering among the poor.

A party of rioters from Drewsteignton attacked the flour mill at Bellamarsh where a fairly large quantity of flour and grain were stored at the time. Joseph Dommett and a party of special constables were hurried to the spot and the vicar at once asked for the ringleaders to be pointed out.

Two men were indicated, named Campion and Northway, the latter being a tall powerful man. Throwing off his coat, the vicar challenged him, and the struggle lasted a full hour, but although the vicar could not subdue him, he could hold him, until more help arrived and the riot was put down.

At the next Assizes, both Campion and Northway were sentenced to be hung, but Joseph pleaded for Northway in Court saying: 'So muscular a man should not be hanged as a felon – it would be a sheer waste, for I could not myself have held him, had he had his belly full'. Northway was reprieved. The vicar was 52 years old at the time of this incident.

He was also a meticulous man, for the bishop's report of that time states: 'The church and vicarage were very well catered for, and ye Sacraments administered six times in ye year'.

Another example of his great strength (recorded by Ellis), concerned a granite gate post in a field close to the vicarage, which had broken off at ground level. The said William Ellis and a Richard Lock went early one morning to start to remove the broken stump, to replace it with a new post; but after struggling with a crowbar and chain for a considerable time, they were unsuccessful.

Ellis then noticed a window in the vicarage was open, and the vicar watching. A few minutes later he came striding over the fields towards them, clad only in trousers and slippers.

When he saw what they were trying to do, he said, 'Put the chain six inches lower and stand back'. He then grasped the chain and with a tremendous heave, broke the suction, drew the stump out of the ground and threw it several feet away – it was three feet long, ten inches in diameter and of solid granite. As he turned to walk back, he was heard to say quietly, 'Nothing but a parcel of boys'. He was 77 years old at the time!

TRANSFER OF THE MANOR

The Manor of Bovey was transferred to the Courtenay family in 1747, who then held it for 110 years. It then passed to the Bentinck family, who were the last to hold the title of Lords of the Manor.

INDUSTRY

About 1790, a woollen mill was in operation at Little Bovey, owned by the farmer. Water to wash the wool was drawn from several ponds on the south east side of Knighton Heath, which were filled with rain water. This ran in channels from the heath to the mill at various levels, being stopped at the mill end and drawn as required. The water from the River Bovey was not pure enough, being contaminated by minerals, especially tin [and also iron - Ed.]. This part of the heath was then owned by the farmer at Little Bovey.

At this time farmers at that end of the parish used a grain mill at Pullabrook because of the high dues called for by the Lord of the Manor, for use of the Bovey Mills which were his property.

In 1766, William Ellis' grandfather went into partnership with a Mr Tufnel, the then owner of Indio, to found the first pottery at Indio House. Craftsmen were brought down from Staffordshire to form the first nucleus of workers, while all the apparatus and kilns were established at Indio House.

The ware was of poor quality at first; using local clay from Heathfield, with kilns fired by the local soft coal called lignite, which did not give a good steady heat. The completed wares were carried to the customers on pannier donkeys. Often the workers had to be paid in kind, in lieu of wages.

Records confirm that there was a pottery at Indio, while in addition in recent years many pieces of broken pottery were unearthed by the excavations, when electricity cables were laid underground to Indio House. [See editors note page 43] It is also on record that Josiah Wedgewood visited the pottery in 1775.

Then in 1790 the Stover canal was started, being built from the head of the Teign at Newton Abbot to Teigngrace, for the purpose of transporting coal and clay from Teignmouth by barge, and thence from Teigngrace to the Bovey pottery by horse and cart. This imported clay and coal made a much better product, but it was a long and tedious transporting business.

The canal was built and financed by James Templer, who lived at Stover House. It was James' son George who conceived the idea of the granite railway. It was built of Haytor granite from the quarries owned by the Templer family. The canal was built in the years 1792/94, by a Mr Gray of Exeter, for James Templer of Stover. Its main purpose was to convey clay by barge from both Bovey and Chudleigh, but it never reached either place, finishing at Ventiford. Much clay and lignite, however, was transhipped along it to Newton Abbot and coal was imported to the Bovey Pottery, being moved from the canal end either way by horse and wagon.

POTTERS FEAST

To return to the Pottery at Indio, Ellis records that the early potters used to hold an annual feast at Martinmas of cooked goose, ale and smuggled french brandy, all of which led to a lively feast.

The method of cooking was traditional; the goose was whole, undrawn and unplucked, rolled and completely covered with a flattened lump of clay so that it looked like an oversize pasty. It was then placed in a zagger (or ware-baking receptacle), and put into the kiln to bake. When cooked, the clay covering could be split and removed in one piece, taking the feathers and skin with it. The 'innards' were removed in one lump and the goose was ready for the feast.

The consumption of alcohol was said to be prodigious; as one old potter put it, 'to quell the quacking of the goose'.

In 1800 it is recorded that agricultural wages were one shilling and twopence per day (6p), plus a quart of cider and a piece of ground to keep pigs. The worker could buy barley for breadmaking from the farmer, at 3/- a bushel, half the price of wheat; wheaten flour was never used by the neighbouring classes.

In 1807 a workhouse was built and opened at Townend, probably opposite the Dolphin Hotel, 'to house the poor of the parish', but this was closed again in 1836 and was eventually sold for £20 and demolished.

An extract from the survey of Devon by Benjamin Donn, 1765.

7
THE VICTORIAN AGE

PARISH LIFE

Some of the following material is taken from books and accounts of the time, some from personal recollections of people who remembered those early times. One of them was my grandmother remembered by many as Nurse Farnes. The early part of this century is taken from recollections of my own parents, relatives and friends, some still living.

The differences in life and life style within those 130 years is almost unbelievable, not so much over the first 80 years but especially in the last thirty. Our parents wouldn't understand present times, our grandparents would find them incomprehensible.

In the mid 1800s the population of the parish was in the region of two thousand, and the town itself was very small, just one long straggly street, with St Mary Street branching off from it.

At the one end, it finished at College the only houses beyond the church being the vicarage and vicarage Cottages. Devon house was just about to be built, while at the other end, Heathfield Terrace was the last building apart from Pottery and Bridge Cottages. St John's church was about to be built, while in the centre of the town, the only buildings to the west of Hind Street were the Baptist church and the house which is now Cromwell House in Abbey Road (former the dentists surgery).

The Pottery was the largest employer. At its heyday its work force was in the region of two hundred. Heath's woodyard employed a large number, while Wyatt's Mill had about twenty workmen. Agriculture was a large employer, many farms employing up to six men. The big houses also employed many people and there were many such houses dotted around the area; Colehayes, Indio, Parke, Yarner, Plumley, Stonelands, Dunley, Pullabrook, Riverside and Cross Cottage, giving work to close on a hundred people between them.

The roads of course were unpaved, just earth and stones. They were quagmires in the winter and rutted and dusty in the summer. There was no piped water or sewage. The church had its spring and well for that end of the town and Mary Street had part of the Ashwell Spring running down to Bladders (known as such from the habit of washing pigs bladders).

Another spring came down in the region of the Town Hall (then still the village green), and ran as an open stream down through Fore Street to the river. These with a variety of wells, were the only sources of water.

The only sanitation was from earth closets. Sinks were emptied anywhere that was convenient, and this, together with the water supply, was deemed to be the source of the outbreak of cholera, typhus and smallpox which was rife in the town at this time. Heating for most people was either by wood or by the local coal, lignite. Lighting was either oil lamps for the upper and middle class or candles for the workers; many of the poorest went to bed as soon as the evening meal was finished. The parish church had chandeliers of candles; I imagine it was the duty of the verger to see to these.

Two of the illustrious sons of the town at this time were Billy Stroud and Walter Tapper. Billy Stroud lived in Mary Street with his sister. He was very fast at mental calculations and but for the fact that he was otherwise mentally unbalanced, could probably have made a fortune. He could calculate anything in his mind in seconds. One example given: he was asked how much a fat bullock, weighing 6cwt 3qrs 14lbs would come to at $4^1/_2$ pence per pound, and gave the correct answer immediately, probably better than our present day computers and calculators could do. Unfortunately, his sister died before him, and he was sent to the Exminster Asylum, where he died. He must have been a man whose calculating feats equalled any of the other prodigies of whom we have heard.

Walter Tapper, whose family were builders (they built part of St John's Cottages) once sang in the choir at St John's. Walter forsook the building trade to become an architect, articled to Mr Rowell of Newton Abbot. He rose to become Surveyor to Westminster Abbey and York Minster, and became president of the Royal Institute of British Architects. He designed the floor of the memorial to Lord Halifax in York Minster, and his plans for Liverpool Cathedral were rated third on the list. He was knighted by the Queen for his work in architecture.

The roads of this era were only muddy tracks and the two to Newton Abbot were quite distinct, the main track via Drumbridges was much as it is now, but the Teigngrace Road began just above the old Toll House and Pound Yard. From there on it was all heathland. In fact it is on record that when St John's church was built the walls of the churchyard were bounded by heather. The track ran behind St John's Cottages, between Indio and the Indio Pond down into Accommodation Road and across into the present Teigngrace Road. Teigngrace Road was not otherwise connected with the

Newton Road as it is now, but carried on through Heathfield to Teigngrace and on to Newton. In 1852 Bovey Bridge was widened to cope with the increased wheeled traffic and if you look up under the arch of the bridge on the Mill side, the mark of the widening can be plainly seen. Unfortunately, no details seem to exist to tell us exactly how this work was accomplished.

The Enclosures Act came into being in 1866, but was illegally enforced long before that. The dire result of which was that the many allotments along the Newton Road which were used by the commoners of the town were gradually taken away, being finally annexed by 1866.

Mr A. J. Wyatt tells us that at a Court Leat of that date, the commoners were plied with much to eat and drink and were then induced to put crosses on a document, thereby giving up their rights to any cultivation. He was told this personally by a Mr George Endacott who lived in Mary Street, opposite what is now the entrance to Crokers Meadow. Mr Endacott's father held the rights to one of these strips of land and being teetotal and sober, he refused to sign the documents thereby retaining possession of his strip. This was still being used and cultivated right up until 1920, the only one to be so retained.

St John's church was built on land that used to be known as 'Teddy Hill'. When the building was first proposed much local feeling was aroused by the rumour that it was to be built on the winnowing field where the townsfolk used to thresh their gleanings. It was in fact to be built on Teddy Hill, on land given by William Courtenay the 10th Earl of Devon, father of Canon Courtenay. This was with the consent of the Court Leat of the Borough of Bovey Tracey and of the manor of Langaller.

The squaring and nobbling of the stone for St John's was done by local stonemasons as overtime, at $3^1/2$d per hour plus cider.

The Congregational church was formed in Mary Street in 1857, the original church being at the back of the Old Manse. Parts of the interior of the old church can still be seen.

The Methodist church building in Mary Street was constructed in 1880 at a total cost of £785, where it remained until the 1950's.

By the latter part of the century life was a little easier. Gas lighting had appeared on the streets and piped water was available from the reservoir in Trough Lane. Water was not piped into individual houses, but to taps set in the outside walls around the town.

Commercial life was strong, there were at least four or five of each of the main types of shops, in fact the town was more or less self supporting. Small businesses abounded; carpenters, builders, ironworks and forges. Wheelwrights were in evidence in all parts of the town. Two very successful businesses were at this time just being founded, Bowdens Foundry and Forge, and Tuckers Carpentry and Wheelwright.

Bowdens employed several farriers and blacksmiths and their reputation spread, both as good trades people and as innovaters of farm machinery. The late Mr Bill Bowden and his father were the inventors of several farm implements that were later patented and sold all over the country. The Tuckers were the makers of carts and carriages as well as being undertakers. Founded by their father, the firm was in 1894 taken over by the brothers Jabez and George. They employed three tradesmen at 6d an hour, three apprentices at 1 shilling a week and several labourers at 4d an hour. All their wood was local and well seasoned before use. Wheels for carriages contained three types of wood, ash for the rims, oak for the spokes and elm for the hubs. All wood was sawn by hand in a saw pit, which stood on the site of Moorlands. The old oak bier used by the church for funerals was made by them in the latter part of the century, and this is still in the possession of the Town Council.

INDUSTRY

In 1836, a Mr Buller and Mr John Divett became the owners of the Pottery, and the new, much larger pottery was built.

When the railway came to Newton Abbot, Mr Divett negotiated for a branch railway, calling a meeting of the towns-people to explore the idea, and raise the capital. In 1866 the South Devon Railway Co. was formed, with two sidings, one for granite brought down from Haytor on the old stone tramway, and one for the Pottery for the import of coal and clay.

The local clay pit at Bluewaters was also in use, and was drained by a water wheel, which also worked the mechanism for raising the clay.

Records of the Devonshire Association speak of an Art Exhibition at the Town Hall in 1868, when good pieces of local terracotta ware were on show. A good export trade was begun, especially to Malta; at one time as many as 60 to 70 crates were despatched from Teignmouth by sailing boat. The Pottery flourished until Mr Divett died in 1885. There is a memorial window to John and Henrietta Divett of Bovey Tracey in the church at Ilsington.

[Editors note: Since the Authors death in 1991 much archaeological work was carried out at Indio House and Heathfield by Mr Brian Adams of the two known pottery sites. A report *Bovey Potteries 1750 - 1836* by Brian Adams gives details of new evidence and gives further reference sources and documentary evidence, relating to the potteries history. In 1993 the glass company, House of Marbles, who occupy the former pottery buildings in Pottery Road held an interesting exhibition relating to the former potteries].

GRANITE RAILWAY

The Granite Railway has been well covered in other books, but their effect on our parish might be mentioned.

The Granite Railway was built by George Templer, the son of James in 1820. It was an engineering achievement in its own right; the rails being constructed of large baulks of granite with grooves hand chiselled out for the wheel flange and complete with complicated point systems. It was laid for the length of 7 miles, and a drop of 1000 feet while the gradient was calculated meticulously to suit the horse hauled wagons. The route of the rails can still be followed for a large part today.

Its journey through the parish of Bovey (See map on page 45) took it down through Yarner, Wisselwell, and Chapple Lane, then down to the back of Pottery Cottages, where one of the surviving mileposts, the 3 mile one, still stands. For a large part of this stretch, the original rails can still be seen, joined up with the Canal at Vetiford and in parts the County Council have undertaken to clean up and preserve them. From Pottery Cottages onwards the route disappears, but it followed the line of the road down to where the old Pottery Bridge was, and from there on it was taken over by the old South Devon Railway, to lay their new metalled track

The ruins of dwellings used by Workmen at the quarries can still be found, while on one of the branch lines leading out towards Hound Tor, a complete small circular hut may be found – whether a hut for living in, or the storage of implements, is not known.

THE OPEN VAULT

Going back a little in time, the Rector who followed Joseph Dommett was the Revd. William Carwithen. During his incumbency, George Clapp of Parke died, and the family vault under the church was opened to receive his body. William Ellis records this as 1822, when he himself was still living in Bovey.

He says that owing to the need for some masonry work on the vault, it was left open for several days, which allowed anyone of a curious disposition, and enough courage, to go in and look around. One thing to be seen was a skull, quite alone, with no sign of the skeleton – the skull of a young man with a full set of perfect teeth, but everyone loose in its socket.

Within a couple of days, every tooth was gone. Apparently there was a local superstition that to possess the tooth of a dead person was a certain preventative of toothache and many of the local inhabitants plucked up enough courage to enter the vault and secure one; though whether this led to a noticeable reduction in toothache in Bovey, is not recorded.

C & J Greenwoods map of 1827. (Note the Haytor granite railway)

Following the Revd. Carwithen, came John Macauley. Then in 1849 came the Hon. Charles Courtenay and with him began what was known as the 'Golden Age' of Bovey.

CANON COURTENAY

Canon Coutenay was the youngest son of the 10th Earl of Devon. He took his degree at Christ church, Oxford, was ordained in 1840 and three years later became domestic Chaplain to Queen Victoria.

In June 1849 he married her Lady in Waiting, Lady Caroline Somers-Cocks, at Buckingham Palace with the Queen and Prince Albert attending the wedding. The following month the Queen appointed him to the living of Bovey Tracey and being unable to fulfil his duties as Domestic Chaplain, he was appointed Chaplain in Ordinary, Canon of Windsor.

SCHOOLS

A little before this, in 1834, a Mr Francis Berry gave a garden adjoining the churchyard to build a school where children would be educated according to the principles of the church of England; he also made a grant towards the cost of £250.

This school, (now known as the Church Room), was first used for both boys and girls, but later in 1864 the Church School on the opposite side of the road was commenced, (now a private house, 'Panorama'), and the boys moved over there, leaving the girls in the old room for a while. Eventually it became vacant and was used by the church, being variously known as the Church Room, Brigade Hall, Church Hall and Parish Hall.

The British School in Mary Street was opened and run by Annie Croker as a non sectarian school to counter the supposed high church leanings of the Church School, to which she was fanatically opposed. This in turn was closed down in 1910 when the council school (now the primary school in Abbey Road) was opened.

Annies' father Dr John Croker of Cross Cottage, was in 1822 experimenting in vaccination for both smallpox and whooping cough. His own papers discovered in Cross Cottage show that all the experiments were carried out on his own children, giving dates of birth and vaccinations, and unhappily, the dates on which many of them died.

Surviving daughters Annie and Elizabeth, were good artists and many of their drawings are the only indication we have of the architecture of the town in the early 1800s. (See page 57)

Annie Croker's British School, 1910

PARKE

There is an interesting and curious legend about Parke, the old house, which was demolished in 1826. One day when the new building had been completed, an old inhabitant of Bovey came to the house and started to hunt around. When questioned by the owner, William Hole, (the grandfather of the late Major Hole), he said 'Whereabouts could this old chamber have been, do you know where it actually was?'

He then told a story of a relation of his, a mason by trade, who with other men had carried out repairs to the old building many years before. They had to knock a hole in one wall and found a hidden chamber behind. There they saw a group of figures sitting round the table with band instruments in front of them, and in their own words, when the air got to them: 'They all valled abroad'. There was no substantiation for this, but Major Hole's own words on telling the story, were, that perhaps the musicians had irritated the then owner of Parke, and he had them walled up.

Parke in the 17th century

QUEEN VICTORIA

To return to Canon Courtenay, he and his wife visited the Queen at Balmoral in 1852, and this closeness to the Queen leads to the legend that the sovereign did at one time visit the vicarage at Bovey. There is no actual proof, but as with all legends there is no real disproof, and there are stories that help to strengthen this.

The conservatory at the vicarage contained a vine which came from Windsor as a gift, a fact confirmed by Miss Wymark Hyde, daughter of the Revd. Barry Hyde, who was vicar from 1908 to 1923. In fact this vine flourished until it was destroyed by blast from a land mine during the second world war. Also in the conservatory, and now preserved among the church possessions, are three inlaid tiles, (not made of local clay) and bearing the initials C.L.C. V.R. and the date 1856 which was the year of the Queen's visit to Dartmouth.

Another version is that the Princess of Wales once stayed in Torquay to convalesce and used to take long carriage drives in the surrounding country, which could possibly have taken her to the Courtenays as family friends.

Most likely the real truth will never be known; but in the early part of this century it was looked on by the older inhabitants of the town as a fact, and the existence of the tiles and the vine are not to be discounted.

In the 1850's, the new vicarage was built in the gardens of the previous vicarage, which stood in what is now the walled kitchen garden and has since been demolished. (This new vicarage has since become a private house, known as Grey Gables).

DEVON HOUSE

In 1863, the work of Mercy of the Clewer Sisterhood, undertaken by the Convent of St John the Baptist, Windsor, was first begun at Bovey, due chiefly to the interest of Canon Courtenay, who was interested in church penitentiary work.

At this time it was calculated that in the County of Devon alone, those needing the shelter of a home numbered many hundreds. The existing homes in Exeter and Plymouth could take but a small proportion of the numbers.

At first, a start was made at Chapple, on the opposite side of the town, which was fitted and equipped for the purpose. Here the first girls arrived, supervised by three of the Sisters. A garret was converted for use as an Oratory, but the initial troubles in running the place were many and hard.

The only sitting-cum dining room had to be used for all occasions including the use of visitors, who came to learn about the need for the work. The house was subject to flooding, especially in winter after a thaw, and the Records state: 'The laundry work, which has always greatly helped the maintenance of the inmates, was necessarily done under great difficulties'. At times the water would come down from the Moor impregnated with copper, so that the clothes had to be re-washed several times. There was no means of drying the clothes when the weather was wet, and great difficulty in heating the irons on the stove.

Moreover, it was distressing that applications for admittance frequently had to be refused, for the house could hold only twenty girls; in 1864 alone, no less than forty had to be refused.

Urgent action was necessary; the Bishop of Exeter appealed to his clergy for funds, and the response was so encouraging that the first stone of the present building, the 'Devon House of Mercy' was laid in 1865 on fields called 'Hill Close' and 'Penny Park', obtained through the good offices of Canon Courtenay.

Four years and seven months after the work had commenced at Chapple, the first occupants moved into the new house, the first completed part being the west wing.

Funds for the start of the chapel were given by one of the Sisters, but thereafter, everything for its completion had to be begged for; we read, 'It was built in the early english style, and contained some excellent painted glass by Hadman and some fine marble work'. The construction of the chapel progressed so well that it was ready for use soon after the west wing was completed; the central section was then built, and finally the east wing.

In the grounds, another building was commenced which was known as the 'Cottage'. This was used as an infirmary, and the probationers' ward, looked after by Magdalens'.

The chaplain's house was also built, just outside the main entrance. In 1872 in the Western Morning News, was printed: 'There were no fewer than 69 inmates in the Devon House of Mercy last week; this large number, though most satisfactory and cheering to those who are interested in the work of mercy, renders them anxious as to the wherewithal to feed so many'.

The house could in fact, on completion, hold one hundred, if the funds allowed. We know that in 1881, owing to a heavy debt on the maintenance account, the numbers of the girls had to be lowered, but the restriction was soon relaxed after the debt was reduced from £623 to £131.

Devon House of Mercy, 1900.

At Devon House there was a remarkable woman in charge – Sister Bertha, who was a Prussian by birth. She came to England as a Lutheran and worked there from the start until a year or two before her death.

Under her, the girls were accepted from the ages of thirteen to eighteen, the younger ones first being trained at the 'Cottage'. There were three main divisions of work – Laundry, Kitchen and Embroidery; while the girls were organised in 'sets', each set having its own dining room and living rooms. No talking at meals was allowed, although individual reading was.

The uniform was blue and white striped dresses, high at the neck and thick white aprons with a cap like a bonnet tied under the chin and thick grey shawls which they pulled over their heads in rain.

Once they had 'got their class' they were promoted to a Sister Dora type of cap.

The girls used to go for long walks for exercise, in crocodiles, supervised by the Sisters. A fact which I well remember in the 1920's and 1930's.

They were always interested in children and would stop and make a fuss of the occupant of a pram, or any youngsters out for a walk, until moved on by the Sister in Charge.

Annual events which the girls could look forward to, were the Christmas play, a party which took place on John the Baptist's Day (Clewers' Patron Saint), the annual sale and strawberry teas in the summer.

Income for the maintenance came from sundry donations and the laundry, which collected and delivered all over the area. While the large kitchen garden, (which was the field between the house and the church), supplied all the vegetable needs.

An extract taken from the Clewer archives states: 'Since the work began in Bovey Tracey in May 1863, six hundred and more poor girls have been under the Sisters' care, of these, upward of 80 are now in the House; nearly 300 have been placed in service, 150 have been restored to their families, 36 have been sent to different homes, 19 have died, and the remaining 41 have either left under medical advice, or at their own request'.

A less well known activity which the Clewer sisters undertook, directly concerned the people of Bovey Tracey itself. The town had a large Pottery in those days, employing men, women and children; by far the largest employer in the district, while there were a large proportion of sick, poor and aged. Half-way down Fore Street, a red brick house was built (by the gift of a benefactor believed to be Canon Courtenay), on the site of the old original Grammar School. It was known as the 'Mission House' and opened in October 1879 and staffed by the Clewer Sisters. [Editors note: This is now know as Courtenay House and is an antiques centre and tea room, although many know it as the old Job Centre].

The Mission House was used as a base for general relief work in the parish, holding confirmation classes and mission services. A large room in the house was used as a dormitory for convalescents, and there was also a chapel.

The two sisters in charge at the time were Sister Lucy Edith and Sister Magdalena, who also ran guilds for the teaching of needlework to young girls of all ages.

A stock of baby clothes was also held there, for the use of the poor, and my grandmother, who was midwife at the time, if she were attending a confinement, and the mother was unable to afford clothes for the baby, would send for a supply from the Mission House – a request which was never refused.

My mother, or her sisters, were often despatched on errands of mercy such as this.

SOCIAL SERVICE

Soon after Canon Courtenay became incumbent of Bovey he wrote a long and interesting letter to his parishioners, explaining all the services of the church. Also stating that he was starting evening school, adult classes, and cottage readings which were to be provided for 'the old and infirm, and women detained at home by the care of young children'.

A District Association was formed, as was a Sunday School clothing club and a lending library; moreover books, bibles and prayer books could be bought at one third of the usual price, and paid for by instalments handed in at the vicarage.

Again from the records, we read the following: 'Any respectable married woman, making application at the vicarage a month before she is likely to want them, can have the loan of baby linen, and things necessary together with a packet of groats and half a pound of soap'!

The Canon was a very generous man — his generosity was well known among the tramps and vagabonds of the day, and it is said that he was much imposed upon.

Believing that if only a small percentage of the tales of woe he heard were true ones, he would not risk turning away a request for money for food and clothing, or to visit a sick relative. But at last he overcame this problem by issuing chits, either for bed and lodge, or for the Station Master to issue a ticket, both redeemable by him. A pity it is not recorded how many of these chits were actually passed for redemption by him!

THE PARISH CHURCH OF ST. PETER, ST. PAUL AND ST. THOMAS OF CANTERBURY AND ST. JOHNS CHURCH

About 1858, a fairly ruthless cleaning up of the parish church began. Some parishioners seemed to believe that the church was spoilt by the galleries and box pews which had been in place for at least three centuries. These and other items were removed and the north asile was added to replace the accommodation removed.

On removing the whitewash from the then north side of the nave, a series of paintings were uncovered which were probably the work of artists of the early 1400's. They showed two groups represented the 'Moralities' known as 'the three living and the three dead Kings', a very popular subject in the fourteenth century; while another two groups illustrated the Judgement and the Power of Prayers. Once they were uncovered these ancient works of art started to fade, but luckily a keen local painter Miss Hole of Parke, made very good copies of them which can still be seen hanging at the west end of the church.

Amongst other articles lost, was the old sounding board, placed there by the Revd. Forbes to help the accoustics. This has been missed more than many people realise.

The cross which is now part of the Courtenay Memorial, was discovered by Canon Courtenay being used as a step into the churchyard. It was rescued by him and set up on the right hand side of the churchyard, from where it was moved to its present position after his death.

The Canon was a high churchman, while the parish church was, as it is now, middle of the road. The parishoners would not hear of any alteration to the services, so he began the building of St John's church, on the site given by his brother, the Earl of Devon.

The building was begun in 1851, the architect being a Mr R C Carpenter. It was completed, and the church consecrated in 1853, as a chapel of ease to the parish church, with a curate to assist in the services.

Quite soon Canon Courtenay took a dislike to the reredos in the church, and commissioned Charles Francis Hansom, who with his brother, Aloyius, were well known Roman Catholic architects (also the designers of the Hansom Cab), to design a new one.

At St John's church the Canon could have his high church services and leave the parish church as it wished, although there were rumblings in the parish. In 1878, wall posters appeared in Bovey headed 'Romanism at Bovey Tracey'; these took the form of a letter to the Lord Bishop of Exeter, complaining that the services at St John's church were no different from those at a recognised Roman Catholic church.

In 1855, in an agreement on the one side between Canon Courtenay, the Lord Bishop and the Earl of Iddesleigh, on behalf of the Crown, and on other side the Wardens and Scholars of Keble College, Oxford on behalf of the Church, it was stated that Canon Courtenay would have the sole right to appoint a Minister to the church, and on his death the patronage to pass to the Wardens and Scholars of Keble for ever (this patronage has since been passed to the Guild of All Souls).

On the death of Canon Courtenay in 1895, the following appeared in the London Gazette of November 29th headed 'At the Court of Windsor'. It presented to the Queen's Most Excellent Majesty, from the Ecclesiastical Commissioners'. We, the said Commissioners, humbly represent that all that part of the said parish of Bovey Tracey, as described in the attached schedule, should be assigned, to the church of St. John, and is to be named 'The District Chapelry of St John the Evangelist' and that marriages, batisms, buriels and churchings may be solemnised there.'

I have a copy of the Gazette, describing this in full, and outlining the boundaries granted. So St. John's became a separate entity, but the parish church still remains as the parish church.

Incidentally, at this time, the house which is now the St. Mary's Church Army Home (behind St. Johns Church) was the country home of the 2nd Lord Halifax, referred to by him as his 'Country Cottage'.

In the Archdeacon's report of 1876 on the parish church, it states: 'the Porch and Lychgate are in a deplorable condition, your tower is shabby, and your clock a delusion'. By 1878 this had been made good and the Lychgate, at the top of the steps, leading to the south door, was demolished. Plans were made for rebuilding it and indeed designs made, some of them very ugly and victorian, but this was never done, which was really a pity; it should have been replaced with a good design.

Also in 1878, the old frame type clock in the tower was replaced by the present one, made by Benson of Ludgate Hill. Unfortunately the old works were destroyed. This present one is weight driven by two weights, one for the clock and one for the strike, which weigh $1^{1}/_{2}$ and 3 hundredweights (75 and 150kg) respectively. These are carried on steel cables and travel from the top of the tower to the floor of the clock chamber, in a week's run. It takes thirty nine turns of a two foot handle for the clock, and one hundred and twenty for the strike, which has to be done weekly.

The clock strikes the hour on the tenor bell, and is unusual for a tower clock in that it is by rack and not the more usual count wheel or locking plate.

WATER WHEEL

In 1854 the building almost always referred to as 'the old Mill' was built (see front cover photo). It never was a Mill, in fact it was built by John Divett as stabling and outhouses.

The water wheel pumped water to a large tank at the top of the tower, which then supplied his house, (now the Riverside Hotel), and the surrounding building (by gravity), thus providing probably the first piped water supply in the town.

It was built on the site of the old Bridge House which was owned at one time by a Noah Flood and so naturally was called the Ark. One of our oldest inhabitants Mr. George Tucker (who died in 1978 at the age of 104) told me he could remember the overflow at the top of the tower, cascading water down over the roof when it got too full.

THE RAILWAY

In the mid 1800's, Mr. Divett, the owner of the Potteries, realised that a better method than horse and cart was needed to supply the business with coal, and take away the finished products.

He called a meeting of the towns people, and explained that unless he had help in this, he would have to close the Pottery. The finance was forthcoming and work on a new railway was started, part of it on the foundations of the old granite railway. It opened in 1866 under the name the South Devon Railway Company, with the station at Bovey, Lustleigh and Moretonhampstead. There were two sidings at the Pottery, one for the works itself and the other to load granite brought down from Haytor.

The original railway had the old gauge of 7 feet, in common with most of the south west; but by 1892, Isambard Brunel accepted the inevitable that the west was to come in line with the rest of the country. On the week-end of 20-22 May, the whole of the South Devon Railway was changed in two days, with the use of thousands of labourers, to the normal gauge of 4 feet $8^1/_2$ inches, as used in the rest of the country.

G.W. Railway Station, Bovey Tracey, 1880.

THE TOWN

All this time (the mid eighteen hundreds), the town was steadily but slowly growing, both in size and in industry. Bovey was a place of many alleys and courtyards leading off the main road; most have disappeared, and only cobbled yards behind doorways remain as evidence, but a few show where they have been. For instance, in East Street opposite the old barn of the Manor, opposite the Town Hall, beside Manns Delicatessen, beside Cobb Cottage (pink painted house) and behind the Old Cottage Tea Shop.

I can remember many places myself, which were still in use in the 1920's. It is a great pity that so many picturesque places have disappeared, when, as in Chagford, they could be places of real interest.

Many of the houses in Fore Street, Mary Street and East Street were built around the 18th century. The Pottery, of course, was the largest employer, taking about 170 workers in all. Farmers and domestic service were the next in size, with many of the large houses in the area taking very many workers.

Life was very hard still, houses being small and very primitive. There was no running water and only oil lamps and candles, with earth closets at the bottom of the gardens. Wages were extremely low, with no paid holidays.

As a comment on the wages of those days, a recording in the Bovey Court Leet Minutes of December 1868 describes a resolution passed: 'That Mr H Payne, the town scavenger, was to be provided with a new barrow and to be paid twenty shillings per annum, to keep the streets clean'. He was otherwise expected to augment his living from the scraps he picked up during his duties!

Roads of course were of earth and stone, worn in by passing traffic, such as horses and carts, causing continuous dust in the summer and muddy ruts in the winter.

TOWN HALL

In February 1865, the piece of land in the centre of Bovey (formerely the village green) and on which stood five dwellings and the market cross and the bull baiting ring and stone, was bought to build the new 'Vestry Room and Town Hall'. It opened in 1866 at a cost of £800; the dwellings being demolished, and the market cross moved to its present position, now being used as a war memorial. The original cross had, many years before, lost its head and was purely a pointed shaft, the present head was presented and fixed through the good offices of Canon Courtenay. Unfortunately, the ring and stone, part and parcel of the horrific sport of bull baiting has long since disappeared.

The Town Hall was built as a result of an Act of 1850, which prevented the holding of vestry meetings in churches and regulated the appointment

Annie Croker's drawing, dated 7 June 1832 , of the green and market cross – where the Town Hall now stands. Beneath the original drawing is a note saying 'Perhaps I see beauty where thou does not.'

of vestry clerks. The piece of land was conveyed to churchwardens 'William Robert Hole and George Slocombe and four others, overseers of the Parish of Bovey Tracey, and to their successors to have and to hold for ever'.

BUILDINGS

Old Market Cross, 1900.

Then in 1874, a plot of land at 34 Fore Street which was a tenement with herb garden, was bought by the Bovey Tracey Temperence Society and in 1877 a Hall was built at a cost of £600, financed by the Independent Order of Rechabites. This Hall is now an accountants office and estate agents.

In 1880 the Methodists built their new chapel in Mary Street, replacing the old one which was a converted dwelling house, (this chapel has since been demolished, for road widening). In 1867, John Divett leased to a party of nine trustees and their executors 'a parcel of ground situated on the north side of Mary Street, to build a British School for the education of the parish children, according to the principles of British Schools (i.e. non-sectarian).

GRAMMAR SCHOOL

In 1875 it was decided to enlarge the Bovey Grammar School. A piece of land was given by Mr W.R. Hole (the father of Major W.G. Hole) at Lowerdown (on the Manaton Road) in 1876.

The school was highly thought of academically, and was for day boys and boarders. It had three free sholarships for local boys who had had at least three years previous schooling and were considered suitable.

The School was built for a total cost of £2,831 3s to which the Hele Charity, (previously described), gave a capital sum of £500 and an annuity of £30. The highest yearly attendance was in 1905 with 35 boarders and 17 day boys. Age limits were 7 to 16 years; fees were £6 per annum for day boys and £25 for boarders. Many of the local farmers' and tradesmens' sons were scholars, some of them riding to school on horseback.

The old Grammar School – now the Edgemoor Hotel.

The school gradually dwindled and it finally closed in 1910, ordinary schools by then being well established. The property was sold by the Governers and the income from the capital sum realised, plus the endowments still received, became the nucleus of the present Exhibition Foundation, of which more will be described later. The old building is now the Edgemoor Hotel.

BOROUGH

In 1883, with the advent of the Municipal Corporation Act, the ancient borough of Bovey Tracey came to an end, after many hundreds of years; the offices of Mayor, Portreeve, Bailiff and Freeholders were abolished and a parish council was formed.

Bovey Tracey was one of the four ancient boroughs in the County of Devon, not officially recognised. With the coming of the new Act, the town officially applied for recognition and for some unknown reason, Queen Victoria did not grant the application, although the vicar of the parish was a personal friend and is wife her former lady in waiting.

The document confirming the abolition refers to 'The late Mayor and late Bailiff' as if it were a kind of death sentence.

The instruments and chattels of the town, the scales, weights, measures for liquids, staves, etc. are in the custody of the Town Trust, stored for safe keeping in the council office.

MAYORS DAY

At about the same date, the ancient and time honoured event of Mayors Day, already referred to, also fell by the way. The feature of the day was the beating of the bounds on horseback, in which thirty to forty equestrians took part. The Mayor was attended by the High Bailiff and two constables, with the Town Band. The town was decorated with flags and arches of greenery, and the whole procession ended at the Mayor's house, for an excellent meal.

Traditionally, the date of the festival was believed to commemorate the wedding day of Matilda de Tracey in the thirteenth century. She was the grand-daughter of Henry de Tracey who was granted the charter for an annual fair in 1260 – a lady who gave to the Freeholders of the Borough large parts of the heath-field for their use for ever.

The mayor and his party would ride three times round the town cross, (it is believed that it was the town cross, so struck, but some sources say that it was the old cross now set in the wall at Cross Cottage); and he would then strike it with a staff to proclaim his authority, after which all the new young freeholders were required to kiss the stone, pledging themselves to uphold the chartered rights and privileges of their borough.

According to the Rev'd. Barry Hyde, this is an example of a boundary monument consecrated by an imprecation, of which there is only one other case in the whole of the United Kingdom; the London Stone in the City of London, which was struck by the rebel Jack Cade in 1450, who struck it with his sword, declaring 'Now I am Lord of this City' as noted in the 'Lord Mayors Court of the City of London.

The custom of electing a Bailiff, Constables and Freeholders still survived up into the 1920s, although of course it had no official status, and was purely social.

I have in my possession a document dated 1925, calling a meeting of the officials, sealed and signed by Harold J Michelmore, Solicitor. Among the names are Bailiff – W H Tregoning, Portreeve – A E Collins, Constables – W Windsor and J Harris, Town Crier and Ale Taster – W Kelly.

CHURCHYARD

In 1874 an addition to the churchyard was consecrated, but in 1890 it was closed by an order of her Majesty Queen Victoria, (save for the Hole family plot).

In the same year the first part of the present cemetery was opened, (after the passing of the burial act), and it was consecrated by the Bishop of Exeter. It has been said in fact, that Bovey Tracey was the first council in the country to open a cemetary after the passing of the Act in 1889.

In 1890, the restoration and re-building of the church organ was completed at a cost of £1000, part of it being purchased from Lancaster Hall in London. At this time the bellows were still worked manually by two strong men.

COURTENAY MEMORIAL

In 1895, after the death of Canon Courtenay, the destruction and demolition of the north side of College was commenced, to provide the present memorial ground to the Canon, with the siting of the old church cross in the centre - its final resting place after many moves and indignities.

The document for the sale of the houses was between the owner, Mary Anne Gale, and the Trustees, John Joll, William Mann, George Bond and Mina Goodwyn, for the sum of £250.

College, about 1890.

Marsh Cottages, about 1890, now part of the lower car park in in Station Road.

WATER

Earlier in the century, in 1869, a general meeting of the parish was called, to discuss a better water supply and drainage system for the town. It was agreed to use pipes of 12 inch and 9 inch diameter.

In 1871, Dr Hayden tried to get this amended to 15 inch and 12 inch, but was defeated; a pity, as the good doctor evidently had the foresight to visualise the growth of the town.

Bovey's main supply of water at the time, was the Ashwell spring which ran down the length of the main street, as an open leat, rather in the manner of Honiton; in this at intervals, there were large holes excavated, called 'dip holes', for the inhabitants to fill their jugs. There were also many wells.

Then in the 1870's the first piped water for the householders was supplied, not to individual houses but in the form of what we would now call stand pipes, at regular intervals throughout the town.

Some of these can still be seen – one beside St. Mary's Well near the church, and one in the wall of Parke View, near the back entrance beside the Old Cottage Tea Shop and some other places. These were still supplied from the Ashwell spring, but via a new reservoir which was built in Trough Lane, and still exists. Incidentally, our four legged friends received their first water supply in 1894 when the Union Square trough was built.

Then in 1901, the council built a much larger reservoir at Trendlebeare, giving the town its own water supply for the next 60 years.

GAS

In 1881, the ratepayers called on the Council to consider lighting the town by gas, successfully requesting a public meeting to discuss this. A private company was formed, and by 1884 gas had been brought to Bovey. Gas street lighting which was soon referred to as 'an extravagance and imposition on the rates'. The old Gas Works was sited on the turning into the old Heathfield Road.

CRICKET

Still in the mid nineteenth century, the site of the present Recreation Ground was given to Charles Aldenburgh Bentinck, the then Lord of the Manor, in exchange for land given up to the Council at Heathfield: 'subject to the obligation of preserving it in good condition and permitting it to be used at all times as a place of exercise and recreation, for the inhabitants of the parish, the owner having the right to pasture sheep there, and the duty to keep up all the fences'.

The Bovey Cricket Club was formed in 1852, and the first match was played in September of that year, the members having cleared away enough of the gorse, heather and bracken to make a pitch in the centre.

The patch was gradually enlarged by the efforts of the club, until today the whole area, almost seven acres, is clear. Bovey can count itself amongst the ten oldest teams in the country, with a ground that is the envy of many.

The cricket team, 1895.

The pavilion was built in 1865 by the cricketers themselves, with money raised by public subscription. The first one was single-storied with a thatched roof. This was later damaged by fire, and the upper storey and a solid roof were added.

The club has many old mementos, photos, bats, etc. on display in the pavilion It is said that right up until the middle of this century it was the regular thing to carry a pocket knife to snip off the growing bracts of bracken if any were seen to be still poking through.

POTTERY

The exact date when the brick and pipe factory of Candy & Co. started at Heathfield is not known, but it is thought it was in the late 1800's. However it fairly soon fell on hard times, and the Fox family took it over as payment of a bad debt. It began to produce glazed tiles and eventually the well known Devon Fires, which soon became a best seller both nationally and internationally.

The Bovey Pottery also was not doing too well. In 1885 Mr Divett died, and his sister carried on the business with the help of her cousin. They tried again, many times unsuccessfully, to fire the ovens with locally produced lignite.

In 1894 the Pottery was virtually closed, but in 1895 a new company was formed and extensive alterations were carried out. Production and trade increased throughout Britain and the Colonies.

JUBILEE

Being a Canon of Windsor, Canon Courtenay had to take part in Queen Victoria's Jubilee ceremonies in 1887, in London. Because of this Bovey was one of the few places which celebrated the event on the Queen's Birthday instead of the actual day; but the Jubilee bonfire was lit on Haytor, from which at least eighteen similar fires could be seen.

DISASTERS

In the latter part of the century, the country as a whole, and the west country in particular, suffered two major natural disasters. In 1891, the great blizzard raged with all the villages on and around the moor being isolated and the countryside buried in snow.

Many of the villages and houses were cut off for at least two weeks; even the railway from Newton to Moreton was blocked for a week with snow packed hard under the bridges, with even the snow ploughs getting stuck. Bovey was without mail for days until the proprietor of the Union Hotel, (now the Cromwell Arms), managed to get through to Newton and back, by a trap drawn by two horses.

There was snow on Dartmoor even until June, while sowing of the land was particularly late that year. The snow was hedge top deep on the country roads, which in many cases could only be used by walking on the hedge tops. My grandmother used to tell many tales of her experiences of that time, as a midwife, being called out and having to walk miles in the snow, on fields and hedges because the roads were impassable.

Then in 1898, the town had one of the worst floods in its history; melting snow, followed by heavy rain, bursting the river banks. Station Road and the Dolphin Square were awash, and the water was half way up the sides of the station platforms. The water was so deep by the river bridge that horses were unable to get through. Pottery workers were unable to get home and were offered hospitality for the night at the Railway Hotel (now the Dartmoor). Livestock had to be rescued from the lower ground and taken to the higher ground of Parke. All the houses in the lower part of the town suffered; the old town mill (now demolished) was flooded and surrounding walls were tumbled, as was a wall by the bridge.

TOWN TRUST

In 1891, the Town Trust came formally into being. The nine trustees and secretary being responsible for the goods and chattels of the late Borough, and the administration of the properties, together with the yearly income accruing. Minutes of the Trust meetings form an unbroken record, back to that date.

So the victorian age drew to its close, with the town developing quite quickly into an independent and far sighted business town. Already thriving and prosperous as a holiday centre, it earned itself the title 'The Gateway to the Moor'.

Heathfield Terrace, 1906

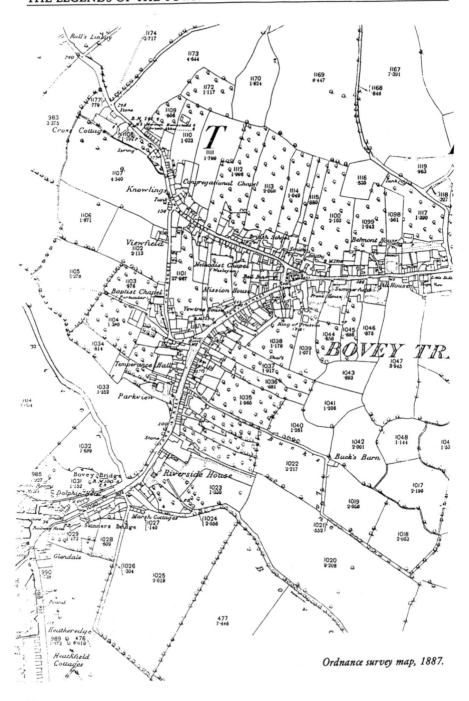

Ordnance survey map, 1887.

8
THE TWENTIETH CENTURY

TRADE

At the turn of the century, it is interesting to note some details; people often say what a good business centre Bovey is, and it certainly is, but in many ways it cannot compare with those days. There were five dairies, five bakers, two gentlemen's tailors, five ladies clothing shops, three shoe shops, three hardware shops, two saddlers, five grocers and many small general and sweet shops; as well as builders, farriers and wheelwrights.

In all it was quite self-contained, and few of the inhabitants ever ventured outside; a trip to Newton was quite an occasion, and as like as not, it was reached by walking. Walking, in fact, was a way of life. Many stories are told of the exploits of people of the time; one man wagered he would walk one hundred miles in twenty four hours, which he did, on a roundabout course – the Dolphin to Chudleigh Knighton, back to Drumbridges, to the Dolphin and round again. Another walked from Newton to Manaton for a wager, in one hour fifty minutes. Long walks to work were commonplace as there was no transport. I myself knew one man who walked regularly from Haytor Vale to Lustleigh to work in the shiny ore mines, leaving home at five to start work at seven, then walking home at night, six days a week.

Also at the turn of the century, the population was about 2,500; today it is between 5,000 and 6,000. The County Directory of the time gives the area of the town as 7,538 acres, and there were 22 farmers named. The Lady of the manor was Mrs Bentinck of Indio, and Henry Trelawney Eve QC resided at Pullabrook.

LEISURE

Entertainment of course was all home produced and included musical and choral evenings. There was a troupe of Black and White Minstrels and other choirs, many of whom used to travel to other villages by wagonette to give concerts. An annual event was the visit of Walfords Welsh Maids, who gave concerts in the Town Hall for about a week at a time and lodged in a house in Fore Street. A character of the time was A. J. Coles, soon known nationally as Jan Stewer, who was a teacher in the town and took part in many concerts.

The annual fairs were still very much a part of life. There were four fairs and markets, at Easter, on 7th July which was a wool fair, on Ascension Day which was a sheep fair and on the first Thursday in November. The one at Easter being best remembered for its stalls of sweets and fairings, one of which was set up at the Town Hall on Easter Monday, where the then vicar the Rev'd. Barry Hyde, used to distribute pennies to all the local children, who could buy a vast range of sweets with such munificence.

MISCELLANY

At this time, the houses at Eureka Terrace and Spion Kop (Mary Street) were built and named as a tribute to the relief of Mafeking; while Mr Cleave and Jim Cummings hauled a cannon to the top of the hill to fire a salute to the same when the Boer War ended.

Many of the old names recur again and again in the old parish registers during the past two hundred years, such as Coniam, Steer, Pinsent, Snell, Gale, Staddon, Gribble, Lambshead, Harris, Mardon, Wills, Tapper, Smale and many of the descendants are with us still.

A group of three cottages stood at the top of Mary Street, (up to the last century this was always known and designated, St Mary Street), where it connects with Hind Street, on the Crokers Meadow Side, stood a group of three cottages, while on the same site was the probable position of the gallows, the Lords of the Manor having the right of the death penalty.

Also at this time, the parish stocks were still in evidence and according to the Rev'd. Barry Hyde in this memoirs, they stood in the churchyard in the ground to the west of the tower. I wonder if anyone knows what eventually happened to them?

FIRE

Up to this date, the only means of fire-fighting in the town was provided by the insurance companies; in our case, the Sun and County companies. Any houses which were insured had what is known as a firemark attached to their wall, giving the name or badge of the company concerned. If your premises caught fire and you were not insured, or even if the wrong company attended the blaze, it was quite likely the fire appliance would ignore your plea. This happened all over the country, and not just in this area.

Fire appliance

As far as I can tell, there are only two firemarks left in the town – one is on a house at the top of Mary Street, just below the high path, while the other is over the front door of a bungalow in the lane adjacent to the Methodists church near the bridge. (This mark was moved from the old Co-op dairy nearby).

In 1904 the passing of a government Act, put the onus for fire-fighting on the local councils. The first council fire brigade was formed, composed of volunteers, and a sum of money was voted by the Town Trust, to help in this. A manual, horse drawn pump was purchased and kept in the fire station, which is now the old peoples day centre, at the rear of the Town Hall.

Twenty four strong men were needed to man the arms of the pump, as well as the firemen themselves. In daylight hours they were called by a maroon, fired by Jim Cummings from the back of his shop, but at night everyone had to be called individually by volunteers running around and knocking them up.

On top of this, the horses were usually kept in stables at the Dolphin. As often as not, they belonged to A. J. Wyatt the miller and these had to be harnessed and brought up to the fire station. In fact, if the horses were out to graze, they first had to be caught! As late as 1920, people living in outlying districts were notified by the parish council, 'that in case of fire, they must provide a pair of horses, to convey the engine to and from the fire.' Many stories were prevalent of the brigade at that time, one of the best known being as follows: A fire broke out in Fore Street one evening, where many of the fire men were quietly drinking, when the call came. One of the members who had embibed a little too well, refused to leave until the landlady provided him with a candle to look for the fire. Another version is that the landlady rushed out to see where the fire was and the locals took advantage of her absence to have free drinks, so that many of them were too merry to man the fire engine.

EDUCATION

At this time, education in the town was provided by the Church School, with Mr William Westwood and Miss M. Kellaway as the Heads; the British School with Miss Lena Kingcome as the Head; an Infants School at St John's; a girls Prep School at the Retreat; and the Grammar School which was still strong at what is now the Edgemoor Hotel.

St John's Infants School, 1910.

RELIGION

Religion was well established with the parish church, St John's Church and the Baptist chapel in its present site. The Methodists had just built their new place of worship in Mary Street and the congregationalists met in the chapel at the rear of the Old Manse, while the Roman Catholics had to make long treks to Chudleigh for their nearest church.

Mary Street, 1900.

POTTERIES

The Pottery at this time was thriving, after a setback. Mr Divett died in 1885, and his sister Miss Divett together with a cousin, tried to carry on running the business. They even installed a lot of new machinery, but by 1894 trade was so poor, it had virtually closed. Then in 1895 a new company was formed and with the new management things steadily improved, until by the start of the new century it was working full time.

Some local clay was still being used which was dug from the pit at Bluewaters, and from pits on the heath between the two roads. Different areas provided different sorts of clay for the various types of ware being produced.

At its height there were at least 16 kilns, with all the various buildings or 'houses' used for the many stages of work involved, from the mixing of the clay to the making of the moulds, decorating, firing and packing.

There were ice pans opposite the main pottery, which were flooded in the winter for the formation of ice. This was then stored in an ice house, where it kept for months. Some of it was sold to the local big houses and fishmongers, etc. long before the advent of refigerators.

There were at least five water wheels built by Mr Divett around 1836 and fed from the pottery pond and together with the leat which formed it (running all the way from Becky Falls), was quite an engineering feat.

Two wheels were at Bluewaters, one for pumping out the water, and one for lifting out the excavated clay. One was at the Higher Mill, of the overshot type, which turned the machinery for mixing the clay; one below the pottery cottages which was undershot; one at the Lower Mill, which was a huge one of 50 feet and overshot but later replaced by two wheels; and one at Warwick Mill, which was used for grinding flint to the various sizes needed. All these were supplied by conduits from the pond. Mr Divett was never one to spend money on engines when he could get water power to provide it.

LIGNITE

Between the turn of the century and the outbreak of the first war, German industrialists became very interested in the lignite deposits here, having had experience in their own country. An imposing work site was built between Warwick Mill and Bluewaters which contained turbines and generators, drills and a laboratory, also all worked by water from the pond.

The object was to explore the commercial uses of lignite and produce montan wax and generate enough electricity to supply both the pottery and the village of Liverton. With the outbreak of the war, many of the work force were interned and that was the end of the project. The derelict buildings with all the machinery were still to be seen on the site when I was a lad.

PRE-WAR VARIOUS

In lighter vein, at a vestry meeting on June 12th 1900, the minutes read: 'Enquiries are to be made respecting the parish bath chair' and the parish bier to be examined, repaired, re-varnished and if possible be made to run straight'. In November of the same year, the vicar, the Rev'd. Vere-Stead reported back: 'The parish bath chair has been returned to the vicarage, where it now remained'. Then on February 6th 1901, it was reported re: the parish bier 'Miss Divett had given the bier for the use of any parishoner, and the repairs were to stand over until the vicar had spoken to a certain Mr Beer about the bier'.

In the early 1900's, the Tracey Almshouses were built in East Street, a gift of the Tracey family, the endownment of which is proving very inadequate for the present day.

[Editors note: At the time the author wrote these words, the Alms Houses were in a sorry state. There were no bathrooms and other problems made them barely habitable. The only income the Tracey Alms House Trust had was some 3.5% war stock and the income from the sale of four acres of hay off Mannings Meadow situated at the rear of the houses.

In July 1989 the Tracey Alms House Trust sold Mannings meadow to a consortium of builders who had planning permission for a housing estate. This windfall of 'a considerable sum of money' resulted in the refurbishment of the existing buildings (already listed for preservation), plus the addition of 3 more new dwellings. They were built to a high standard and completed in 1993. In addition, an endowment was set up by the trust which enables the occupiers to live rent free inclusive of light, heat and hot water. The only costs to them being water rates. At the time of going to press the building of a housing estate, for which Mannings meadow was purchased, had not yet been started].

In 1902, the six bells of the parish church were re-hung, with the addition of two more, to bring the peal to eight; these were the generous gift of Mrs Marion Croker. To help the cost of re-hanging, a two day fête was held at Parke. One of the items which proved very popular at the fête were motor car rides at one shilling a time, from Parke to the Potteries and back in Doctor Goodwyn's new motor car, the first to be owned by anyone in Bovey. The good doctor cut a very resplendent figure making his rounds on his horse, but his car was not so reliable, constantly breaking down on hills and it was a long time before the cause was discovered. It was traced to a loose washer in the petrol tank, which kept slipping over the outlet on going up hill, and so cut off the petrol supply.

The Dartmoor Electric Supply Co. was formed in 1908, with a capital of £3,000. The main generating station was at Mrs Hellier's Mill. Water rights were secured near the Dolphin Hotel, which would keep the price of electricity reasonable; customers were to pay according to the size and number of their lamps!

Some of the church records of that time make fine reading. The total insurance premium for the church was £18, over £600 in 1983 [and now over £1800. The fee for a marriage after Banns, was two shillings and sixpence, plus two and six for the reading of the Banns, but I am sure that even these expenses seemed heavy then.

At this time, the old Rectorial Tithe Barn next to the Church School was still standing, but all that now remains are two of the walls; the age of these is great, but indeterminate.

The first telephone system was installed in 1908. This was completely manual of course and the manual exchange was situated in Station Road, in the business premises of Mr A. Jefferies, where it remained for the next forty years. The telephone numbers were much easier to remember in those days, none of them being more than three digits, many only two. [Editors note: Lustleigh and Manaton still have only three digit numbers].

EXHIBITION TRUST

In 1910 the Exhibition Foundation Trust was formed, out of the demise of the Grammar School. With the funds obtained from its sale a trust of eleven governors was formed. The object of the scheme, which still exists, was to provide funds for grants for school children, to help them extend their further education; the grants to be given on a yearly basis. One of the original governors was Ambrose Godsland, the well known local baker, and great-nephew of our great chronicler, William Ellis.

HAWKMOOR

The grounds of the Hawkmoor estate, (Hauocmore of the Domesday book), were purchased by the County Council in 1913, in the parish of Bovey. The first temporary accommodation for twenty tubercular patients was soon open, and by 1915, so were the first permanent buildings.

The hospital grew rapidly in size and expertise and soon became the main sanatorium in the whole of the county of Devon for the treatment and re-search of tuberculosis. The hospital church was built and consecrated soon after the hospital was started and became part of the ecclesiastical parish of the parish church. [Editors note: Hawkmoor Hospital was closed in the 1980's and the land sold for re-development. At the time of going to print no de-velopment has yet been completed].

THE GREAT WAR

The Great War was a great burden on the people of the town, which was denuded of its menfolk. It is not known exactly how many men served their country, but the Church School had an inscribed scroll of all those old boys from the school who served, and that alone lists one hundred and ninety; so that in total, it must have been at least four hundred.

Fifty five gave their lives. There is a window in the parish church which is probably unique, in that it contains fifty five diamond panes – each one containing the initials, the date he fell, and the regimental badge or name of the ship in which he served, for every man. The window was erected by Drakes of Exeter, as a gift from the sorrowing townpeople.

During the war, people (including troops stationed in the town) objected so strongly to the name of one of the local inns, 'The King of Prussia', that it was re-named the Heavitree Arms. It was known as this until after the last war, since being re-named back to the original. The present inn sign depicts the famous smuggler of Prussia Cove in Cornwall.

BUSES

After the War, the first omnibus service from Bovey Tracey to Newton Abbot was started and at first there were several competing companies, leading to many cut price competitions; but on May 19th 1923 there is the first record of a service by the Devon General Bus Company, with a timetable showing six services each way, on every day, but not including Sunday.

The buses were at first mainly 'Y' type Daimlers and some of them were the open char-a-banc type. They had an average speed of 20 m.p.h. and were known to the local lads as 'Deb'n Kickers', for their boneshaking abilities.

Fares then were ten pence return (4p), seven pence single, with a workmen's return ticket before 8 am of eight pence; and these prices remained fairly static until the end of the 1940's.

In 1905, the Bovey St John's Football Club was formed, very successfully, under the direction of the vicar of St John's, the Rev'd. Wickham. Its playing field was a field by the river, reached by Bucks Lane, and a youngster used to be kept on permanent watch, to retrieve balls kicked into the river which often happened. Before this rugby was the local game. [Editors note: Bovey Rugby Football Club was re-formed in 1992, and play on a field by the river and by-pass]

VOLUNTEERS

A local company of army volunteers, part of the 5th Devon Regt, to which a large number of local men belonged, was still in existence at this time. This was a traditional service which was started on April 25th 1798, when a meeting was called in the then school room, (probably part of the old Grammar School), when a Corps of Infantry was formed.

HOSPITAL

A hospital had existed in the town for many years, the very first being in Heathfield Terrace, then for a while in Marlborough Terrace, and finally for some years in Mary Street, where it eventually became too small to fulfil its requirements. In the late 1920's a committee was formed to plan the building of a brand new purpose-built hospital

The site was acquired, and all the fund raising activities set in motion. The money was raised in total from purely voluntary means, two of the larger subscribers being Mr A. B. Dahl and Dame Violet Wills, who despite her connection with the well known Wills Tobacco Company, had a strong aversion to smoking.

Dr Jack Harrison was brought in as a consultant on the plans, in the hope that he would accept the post of resident surgeon; and he, together with Dr Frank Arnott, the local family practitioner, vetted and approved the plans, which included one of the most modern and up-to-date operating theatres in the county.

The foundation stone was laid in 1931, and the Hospital, originally a single storied building, was opened in May 1932 by Mrs Trelawney. Matron Gunthorpe was in charge of the Hospital until her retirement in the 1960's, and a very happy and efficient unit it was, and still is to the present day. Joe Bezley the local bank manager, was the honorary secretary for many years, administering the hospital capably in his spare time, with the help of a local committee.

Since the early nineteen hundreds the hospital had been financially supported by the annual hospital carnival. At first this was a night time event, complete with illuminated floats and a torchlight procession, (headed of course by the Bovey Tracey Brass Band), but later became a daytime summer event, until the outbreak of the second world war.

Later, in the 1930's, the Spion Kop carnival started as well, run by Mr & Mrs Bill Blackmore, which was held on November 5th starting and finishing at Spion Kop, in the field above Blackmores' dairy, with fireworks, and cheese and cider.

After the second world war, of course, the newly formed National Health Service took over the Hospital, but the voluntary tradition is still carried on by the League of Friends, who every year raise large sums of money for the comfort of patients, and to purchase expensive items of equipment.

EXPANSION

Just a little earlier, in 1929, the Crokers Almshouses were built, through the generosity of Mrs Marion Croker, on a site just in front of the Hospital; while the Almshouse Trust was combined with the Town Trust to oversee the running of the houses.

In the 1920's, two smaller potteries came into production in Bovey – the Devon Tors and the Devonshire potteries, but both of these, alas, together with the Bovey Pottery are now closed.

About 1925 a scout troop was formed by Reg Hodge, the town hairdresser, and this proved very popular with the local boys, especially the many camps held, both locally and on holiday. Later a rover troop was also formed, headed by George Treen, and this continued until the outbreak of the second world war.

FIRE

The Fire Brigade up to this time, was still a horse drawn manual pump. In 1927 the Council purchased a motor fire engine, a hard tyred Stanley Ford, which incorporated a motor pump and an overhead ladder, a vast improvement on the old one. The Chief Officer at this time was L. S. Mardon, and Second Officer A. J. Coombes.

The maroon was still in use as the method of call out by day, but night calls by messenger were the only way after dark; after the war, the air raid siren on the roof of the town hall was operated by remote control to call the men, and Bovey was one of the first places to have this form of call out. The call-out now is by individual radio.

In 1935, the 'Queen Mary' was bought for the town by public subscription, and was christened in the Union Square by Dame Violet Willis, with water from the fountain. This was a much improved modern engine, where the men could sit down on going to a fire (This engine was recovered by Mr Geoff Wills and his son for restoration). This was in use until the 1960's and attended very many fires, including those of the Plymouth blitz during the war.

DISCOVERY

In 1934, during excavations near the site of Pixie Corner the newsagents in Fore Street, a mediaeval oven or kiln was discovered, its age estimated at around 1660. The Western Morning News of March 28th 1934 contains the following account: 'An old kiln and collection of vases was discovered yesterday during excavations on a building site at Bovey Tracey, the pottery included semi glazed vases and a bomla water vessel'. For a while this oven could be seen inside the works gate at Candy and Co. of Heathfield. To what pottery it belonged, or where it came from, nothing is known.

ROMAN CATHOLIC

The Roman Catholic parish at Bovey Tracey was shared between Buckfast and Newton from 1904, with services being held in a little corrugated iron church, situated opposite Moor View, Mass being said regularly by priests residing in the locality. Then in 1929, Father McLachlan was sent to Bovey for health reasons, and determined that the little tin church of St. Catherines was inadequate. After many financial difficulties, and hindered by a cautious bishop, but greatly helped by Mr A. B. Dahl, the foundation stone of the present church of the Holy Spirit was laid in 1935, to form what is now the Roman Catholic 'parish' of the area, which includes Lustleigh, Ilsington, Manaton, North Bovey, Hennock and Moretonhampstead.

LIFE IN GENERAL

Wages were still very low, between two and four pounds per week; but though times were hard, there was a great sense of community life. Food, in the main, was nothing like as full or varied as it is now – one good roast meal a week, with the rest of the week using up the 'leftovers' in stews and hotpots, and fish of course, which was cheap.

Vegetables, however, were plentiful and almost every household had its garden or allotment. I well remember old Joe Gribble going round with a hand cart, selling swede turnips at a halfpenny each. I also remember many of the local homes where it was a case of bread and margarine, or bread and jam, but not both at the same time.

In the 1920's of course, traffic was very sparse, and children going to school could quite safely play their games in the road – marbles, hoops, tops, skipping, etc. – with no fear of being knocked down.

One of the means of entertainment for children in those days were pageants, mimes and plays, being tirelessly arranged by ladies from the town; two of whom I well remember from my own boyhood, Miss Ivy Upham and Miss Florie Allen.

SECOND WAR

At the outbreak of the second world war, the Clewer sisters were evacuated from Devon House, never to return, and the building was requisitioned by the military; first of all by British troops, and later by the Americans.

A land mine fell behind Devon House in 1940, (according to local lore, more by accident than design), blowing out the east window of the church and damaging the organ, while by some freak the blast travelled right down Fore Street, blowing out windows on the south side of the street, and not touching the other side. The crater from the bomb can still be seen, as a large round pit at the rear of the buildings in the field; this, together with a couple of machine gunning episodes was all that Bovey suffered physically during the War.

In 1940 Parke was made the Brigade Headquarters of the British Troops in residence, and one of the stories that Major Hole was fond of telling concerned this: on one occasion the band was playing outside, and the band master was standing where once had been a rose bed. Seeing the Major smiling, one of the officers asked what the joke was, and was told that not long before, they had arisen one morning to discover that overnight the rose bed had disappeared down an unknown well, and naturally he was wondering if the band master was going to do the same.

The immediate surrounds, Knighton Heath and Heathfield, were covered in huge sprawling American camps, (the old concrete bases of the Nissan huts can in many cases still be seen); while at Stover was built the American hospital, which has since become the Polish Camp. [Editors note: Now a residential home for the elderly].

Just prior to the war, the town really started to grow. Brimley Park and Brimley Vale being completed then; but at the end of the 1940's the real explosion started. Cromwell's Way and all the private estates being completed since then, more than doubling the population.

POSTWAR

In my own lifetime I can remember when the town finished at the parish church, and there were only a handful of houses beyond St Johns, while to the west of Hind Street, it was all fields and orchards.

In 1959 came the closing of many of the branch railway lines in Devon. On 2 March that year, the Moretonhampstead passenger service was discontinued with the stations at Moreton, Lustleigh and Bovey being closed. For a while, freight was carried as far as Bovey, mainly in bulk coal and animal feeds, but by the mid 1960's even this was closed. It is hoped that before long, part of the route of the disused line will be part of the Bovey by-pass. [Editors note: In 1987 the by-pass was opened, relieving the traffic going through Bovey on the Moretonhamstead route. The route of the old railway was used, in part, from Pottery Road to just before the crossing of the river Bovey at the new Hole Bridge – where the old track dives off to the left into what is now National Trust land of Parke, and a popular walking route].

At the close of the war, a company headed by Mr Parish, acquired the rights to work the old disused lignite works at Bluewaters, becoming the British Lignite Co. It was hoped that massive use could be made of the by-products, in plastic, wax, etc. After a period of great activity and excavation, with Devon House being purchased and turned into flats for employees, the project foundered.

Also at the close of the war, the local branch of the St John's Ambulance was formed, several founder members being already members of the Newton Abbot contingent. In 1948, a well equipped modern ambulance was purchased by voluntary contributions and staffed by local volunteers, only for it to be taken over in September of that same year by the newly formed N.H.S.

CHARTER

One of the outstanding events of the next few years, was the celebration in 1960 of the seventh centenary of the charter granted to Henry de Tracey. This was researched by Lt. Col. B. St. J. Storrs, who was one of the instigators of the celebrations, and during that year, the whole town came to life and became history conscious.

A pageant was held in July, in which over 200 inhabitants took part. The Marsh field became a mediaeval township, where all aspects of Bovey history were depicted; while historical displays were mounted in various halls in the town as well as in the parish church. Press cuttings and photographs of the time show how wholeheartedly the population entered into the spirit of the occasion.

CHANGES

One other large scale operation that benefited Bovey was the formation in 1966 of a swimming pool committee which was formed to provide a pool for the town. This was built by volunteers, and after a great deal of hard work, opened in 1971 with Ron Harris as its first Chairman. Together with many improvements it has functioned ever since, to the great benefit of the town, and at no costs to the rates.

Many improvements have also been made to the parish church, and these are noted in the church guide. In truth the town is still progressing forward, with a major event being the gift of Parke to the National Trust, on the death of Major Hole in 1974, and many walks and picnic areas being formed, while large parts of the grounds are open to the public. The house itself is now the Headquarters of the Dartmoor National Park, with an enquiries office and a park information centre, while in the grounds is a rare breeds animal farm, a welcome addition to the amenities of the town.

So we come to the end of our story, except for the legends which follow and are numerous. It is often said that we walk about our heritage, in ignorance of its history; but I hope that this little story will, in the case of our town at least give pleasure to people, add to their knowledge, and at the same time record for posterity the story of a town and its people, going back at least 1500 years, and which should be remembered by our successors for many centuries to come.

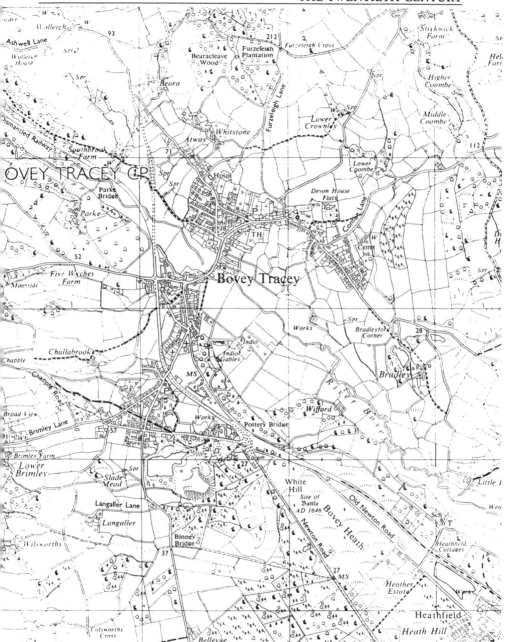

Reproduced from the 1989 Ordnance Survey 1:25000 Pathfinder map with the permission of the Controller of Her Majesty's Stationery Office, © Crown copyright.

9
THE LEGENDS
OF THE TOWN

These are many, and most have their roots in saxon times. Some we have already heard, as part of our history, but others are purely legend; even so, most legends have a base in truth and can be traced to factual happenings, just as ours can.

JOHNNY CANN'S CAVE

The first of these is the legend of Johnny Cann's Cave. This was situated traditionally, in Furzeleigh Rocks, about a mile above the town (reached by Furzeleigh Lane). It was a cave set amongst masses of granite rock, and was pointed out to interested visitors until the end of the last century. Since then, a lot of the stone has been removed for building or other purposes, but Roman coins were discovered at the site, and from memories handed down it is certain there was a cave, and that a hermit lived there. (Incidentally, it is from this cave that Johnny Cann's Walk gets its name). About seven hundred years ago, a young man of an ancient house in Normandy, by the name of Johannes Cannes, was in love with a maiden, also of that area. She was a daughter of a wealthy baron; but unfortunately a deadly feud existed between the parents of the lovers and romance was impossible. The father of the young maiden, (of the house of Drago), had placed her in a convent, and being aware of the romance, intended to send her to a religious house in Derbyshire, via the port of Dartmouth. Johannes came to hear of this through a friend, a monk at the convent. He wrote a letter to the young lady, saying he would join her at Dartmouth. She was to feign an illness and stay at an inn where he would find her.

After a terrible rough passage, our heroine really was ill and stayed at the Saracens Head Inn in Dartmouth, where Johannes, after landing at Brixham, joined her for her convalescence. With the aid of his friend the monk, he obtained a marriage licence and they were married at Christmas time in Dartmouth church.

Once the young bride was restored to health, they decided to make their way to Chumleigh, where Johannes had a friend, John de Garland, who already had an estate in Normandy, and who he hoped would buy his estate from him also. They travelled by pony, (accompanied by the young monk, as he was travelling to Cowick, near Exeter), and used the route Totnes, Ashburton and then on to the Benedictine monastery at Indio, where the monk had friends. After a stay of some days, they departed via the monastery at Hind Street, where they were given the directions to Bridford via Furzeleigh Lane. (At that time the lane continued on from Southbrook Lane, up from Atway to join the present lane above Whitstone, and when Furzeleigh Cross now in the wall at Cross Cottage, really stood on a crossroad.)

As they climbed the hill, the sky darkened and a terrible snowstorm burst on them in full fury. They took refuge in the rocks in the woods above Whitstone, and found a cave where they rested for the night, collecting wood, and lighting a warm fire. They spent a comfortable night, but in the morning the lady was unwell and soon had a high fever (the journey was taxing her more than her husband had realised), and the worried monk started for the village of Bovey Tracey to obtain help and medical supplies.

While he was gone, the bride came out of her delerium for a while and begged of Johannes that if she died, as she was sure she would, she would be buried by the cave, and that in years to come, he would be buried there as well; and that he, although he could not see her, would always feel her presence there. She begged that her friend Bernard the monk consecrate the ground for them.

At length the monk returned with the village doctor, who saw that she was too ill to be moved and that the odds were against her recovery, but enjoined that she might have the best of care. After the physician left, the monk read the consecration office and it is probable that this was the first time that a cave had received such a consecration. After a restless night, she awoke and sadly she would soon be no more; quietly the monk said the last Offices for her, and a Mass as she passed away.

The Squire of Whitstone gladly gave permission for the entombment by the cave, which was conducted by the parish Priest, assisted by the brethen from both Hind Street and Indio; and according to tradition many villagers attended the ceremony, which was held outside the cave one hour before sunset.

The young man, Johannes, determined that he would never leave the spot and became a hermit, living in the cave, serving the needs of the neighbourhood, both as physician and philanthropist to the villagers, many of whom he restored to health and strength. Whenever the monk came, he would always stay at the cave, and this went on for half a century, until, on the 50th anniversary of his wife's death, Johannes too fell ill and passed away. He was buried beside his wife outside the cave, the ceremony being conducted by his old friend Bernard, and ever since this spot has been known to the locals as Johnny Cann's cave.

THE ASHWELL SPRING

Another of the local legends is probably connected with the last one, as it concerns a hermit living in a cave off Furzeleigh Lane, probably Johannes Cann.

There was a custom connected with the Ashwell Spring, that was observed until at least the middle of the last century. On the Sunday before Easter, the youth of the town, of both sexes, would parade to the spring, and there drink sweetened water, ostensibly to ward off diseases of the skin, but chiefly with the object of finding a life partner. The maiden would offer the cup of sweetened water to the boy of her choice, who would accept with a kiss which would often lead to marriage.

William Ellis himself states that he took part in these ceremonies, during the earlier part of the last century, and the custom lingered on for quite a while after this.

The legend runs as follows:

At the time of Johannes Cann there lived at Whitstone, a beautiful girl. She was the daughter of the Squire, who had become acquainted with the hermit during her morning walks, and used to visit him for instruction of all kinds as he was a man of letters, had some skill in medicine, and was known to have treated many of the sick among both the poor and wealthy of the district. One such was a young knight, a resident of neighbouring Crownley, who was enamoured of the young lady from Whitstone, unknown to her, as she was also to him. He had been treated for some time for a slight illness and was almost cured.

Then one day something happened which put a stop to all thoughts of romance; she awoke one morning and found, to her horror, a form of skin disease on her arms, which in those days was terrible to contemplate.

She had no mother or sister to confide in, so after a little hesitation, hurried to the cave of the hermit, where he, seeing her great distress, at once asked her what was the matter. She bared her arms and pointed to the white spots on both arms near the elbow joints, imploring him to tell her if it was leprosy. He carefully examined her and was able to comfort her and say it was not, but a case of salt-rheum, (a vague term in those days for conditions of the skin), and that he was confident that, with the blessing of God, he would soon restore her to a healthy condition; the white spots would disappear and her arms be free from blemish.

He told her to return the next morning, by when he would have procured the necessary roots and herbs to prepare the medicine, and she departed with a lighter heart.

Soon after the young lady had left the cave and the hermit was preparing to go and find the roots and herbs he required, the young knight from Crownley appeared. After a little hesitation, the hermit decided to tell the young man of the girl's disease. The knight became alarmed as he loved her from a distance, but on being assured that she could be cured, he willingly helped the hermit search for the necessary herbs he needed for a decoction, and an ointment of herbs and lard.

The next morning, the girl thankfully received the medicine, one part to be taken internally and the other rubbed on the affected parts. In addition, the hermit, knowing of the feelings as yet untold, of the maiden for the young man, and vice versa, gave her a small pot of honey, and told her to go at noon every day to Ashwell Spring, take with her a small pitcher, put therein a certain quantity of honey, fill the water from the spring, stir well and drink. He told the young knight also to have honied water for his health, and the next day they both met at the spring, as they had been directed.

The following day was Palm Sunday, and after church they both made their way up to the spring, where with some trepidation, the young man told her of his love, and that he hoped it would be returned by her. For her answer, she gave him her pitcher to drink from and said she returned his love in full.

They decided that, with her father's permission, they would be married in twelve months time, after another Lent; and so they were, on the Thursday after the following Easter, with the good wishes of the whole village. They both had a long and happy life together, and were great benefactors to the populace as a whole.

For 600 years after this, the young people of Bovey met and drank sweetened water, ostensibly to improve their health, but more likely to find a life partner, on every Palm Sunday at Ashwell Spring.

This legend survived certainly until the last century, for it is on record that the landlord of the Bell Inn in East Street, (which in those days was situated between Churchill House and the Bovey Court Garage, or Tuckers Garage as it used to be known) who was a crabbed old man nicknamed 'Old Horney', would on every Palm Sunday after Mattins, take a party of young people up the hill to the Ashwell spring to drink water mingleed with honey, 'to ward off infections of the skin, and to give a clear transparency to the complexion.

William Ellis has recorded that he took part in the ceremony on several occasions.

The spring has now been covered over, but the water is still running, and until a few years ago, found its way into St Mary's Well by the church.

THE LEGEND OF PARKE AND THE WHITE RABBIT

At the time of the birth of the legend, Parke was situated as it is now, but was an ancient demi-castellated building, and was the manor proper of Bovey. The time was at the period of the early Crusades, the avenue of beech trees along the drive are said to be the fourth planting since then, which tells its age to within a century or so.

A young and beautiful daughter of the baronial house of this time, was secretly enamoured of a young knight of meagre fortune, and plighted her troth, unknown to her father. The young knight, supposing his love was secure, enlisted under the banner of Richard, Earl of Cornwall, and went off to fight in the Crusade against the Saracens. During his absence, a rival in the person of a young and wealthy baron appeared, and he, although aware of her previous love, thinking only of the honour and wealth that would accrue from a marriage with such a noble family, pressed his attentions with the fair lady, and asked her hand of her father, in the proper manner. While he, thinking of a high alliance of a wealthy baron, counselled her to marry him, and she, although protesting against it, was over-ridden by her father, and the marriage was fixed for June of that year.

She, in the meantime, had had news, (wrongly it later transpired), that her lover had died in the Holy Land, and now unconcerned as to her future, had yielded to the commands of her father. On the very day that the marriage was solemnised in the parish church, the young knight returned from the Crusades, and hastening to the house was greeted by the sound of festivities. The guest were assembled in the upper hall; the young man enquired of the servants the reason for the festivities, and, on being told, sprang up the stairs, thinking she had deceived him and cursing her for her perfidy.

She recognised the voice of her lover, and flew towards him, but he spurned her with a curse and sought for the baron to get his revenge. She, distraught at his action, gave him a bewildered, distracted look, and ran headlong down the stairway, heedless of caution, and at the same time drawing a stiletto from her bosom, (concealed there for a purpose known only to herself), she ran with all speed across the lawn towards the avenue, until she reached the rustic arbour where she and the young knight had first declared their love.

He, sensing what was wrong, turned and ran after her, followed by the husband, and made straight in the same direction, in time to see her fall to her knees in her white wedding dress, in front of an effigy of the Virgin Mary, and press the stiletto to her breast. As the young maiden fell to her knees, hearing her persuers behind her, she cried: 'My love, it was for you I concealed this, and my love is stronger than death, as this friend shall testify,' and lifting her eyes to the statue of the Virgin, she exclaimed: 'Holy Mother, pity and forgive this poor child', and before either of her persuers could stop her, she pressed the dagger into her breast and fell back on the seat, looking as one in a peaceful sleep.

The young knight was first on the scene, and as the baron approached, he felled him with a blow from his fist, then turning to the lifeless figure, kissed her and snatched the dagger from her breast, swearing to use it on the villain who had caused the tragedy. In the meantime, the baron had recovered from the blow, and escaped back to the house for help. The knight also hastened back, untied his horse and rode slowly down the drive, taking a last long look at the arbour, before riding down the avenue.

His horse showed signs of restiveness, and he soon heard the clatter of hooves, so he reigned in his steed and waited, with his sword in his right hand, and in the left the fatal dagger. A voice from the advancing party called 'stop and answer for your dastardly act', and the knight seeing that three others were with the baron, plunged forward at once, drove the dagger into the baron's heart, and with one almighty blow from his sword, decapitated him. He did not immediately fall, but sat as if alive, and was at once supported by his servants, who led the body on the horse back to the house, while the knight rode off down the avenue, fully satisfied with his revenge, a sad end to an ill starred wedding.

It is said that on every anniversary of the wedding, (in the month of June), the upper hall is filled with ghostly guests, until the hour of midnight when they all disappear, and a lovely white rabbit is seen running to where the old arbour used to be, and a ghostly headless figure, mounted on a big black horse, can be seen galloping down the avenue.

William Ellis describes how, when he was a boy in the early 1800's, old people had then told him how they had seen the disembodied spirits, the headless horseman and the lovely white rabbit.

A LEGEND OF THE OWNERSHIP OF PARKE

This is vouched for in old writings of the Courtenay family, of which I have a copy, as well as in the recollections of William Ellis.

In 1702, William Stawell, the proprietor of Parke, died without heirs, and the property passed into Chancery, from which it was bought by a Mr Bale, from whom it was again purchased by John Langdon in the late 1730's. He had already purchased the manor of Bovey Tracey. He married the sister of Sir

William Courtenay of Powderham, and settled at Parke, where they had one daughter, who tragically died in 1747, at the age of 5 or 6. In the meantime, John Langdon's mother had married again, a Mr George Hunt, a lawyer. He proceeded to take over the business affairs of his son-in-law, when he lost his daughter and lost all interest in the estate.

Parke was soon given to (or came into the possession of!) Hunt and Langdon's mother. On John Langdon's death, his widow was cruelly ejected by Hunt, and she only disputed possession for nine months after his death. Hunt had two daughters by Langdon's mother, who became coheiress of Parke, and the manner of their inheritance was to be decided as follows:- the daughters were to provide two candles as nearly alike as possible, and of the same wax or tallow. At the time appointed they were to light the candles at the same moment, and the owner of the one which burnt out first was to have Parke.

William Ellis goes into great detail on the thoughts of the two sisters, as they watch with trepidation, the guttering candles. Whether the winning daughter was the elder or the younger, we do not know, but she afterwards married George Clapp, Esq., and became the mother of the celebrated Councillor George Hunt Clapp. In 1824, the widow of Councillor Clapp sold Parke to a Mr Gold, who in turn, sold it one year later to Mr Hole of Stickwick, the grandfather of Major W. G. Hole, the last owner.

THE LEGEND OF INDIO PRIORY

This was also recorded by William Ellis at the beginning of the 19th century. Indio was originally a priory, probably started before the 8th century, and remained so until the time of Henry II. It then became a Nunnery, under the superintendance of a Prioress; this was said to be due to the influence of Thomas á 'Beckett, whom tradition says had a bishop's Chamber in the old Manor House in Bovey and probably this influence was so. The Nunnery was dissolved in the reign of Henry VIII, and became a private residence about the time of the beginning of the reign of Elizabeth I. Whether the present building is part of this is not known for sure.

Between Indio and Grey Walls lies the pond which was always well stocked with fish. At the time of the Nunnery it was known as the Pond Garden, and used for the relaxation of the Nuns. As with many religious houses of such an early date, the inmates were not 'cloistered' or living in retirement, but were active in welfare, education and the furtherance of Christianity, from which it received its original latin name 'Indeo', a house for, or according to God.

According to tradition, the estate was not richly endowed. There were only ten acres of Glebe attached, and the expenses were met by the production of high class needlework, the productive garden, and the paying members of the school. It seems a young orphan maiden was being taught at the school, and after several years she became so proficient at needlework, that her fame spread and she became the mainstay of the institution.

Among the youths in the male department of the school was the only son of the Lord of the Manor, well liked by his fellow pupils and teachers. He soon fell in love with the fair, but poor, young orphan, and one summer evening they pledged their troth while on a boat ride on the Pond Garden. Soon after the old Lord died and the young scholar became Lord of the Manor and emplored the young maiden to become his wife right away. She readily agreed, but tears filled her eyes and, astonished, he asked why: she explained that the sisters would lose all their profits that came from her labours, and they only had ten acres to crop. 'Then I will give them ten times more, and enclose it permanently', he said, and it is interesting to note that as from that date, the estate was always passed, in conveyance, as 110 acres.

The young Lord threw up a double hedge on three sides of the property, terminating at the river bank, and, as a further act of kindness to the Nuns, he built a double hedge from the Nunnery down to the river, a bridge across the river, and a further path up to the road before the church, to shorten the journey to the church for them. The only part of this path that now remains, runs at the back of Coombe Close; the remains of the bridge can also still be seen by the river.

THE LEGEND OF FROST CROSS AND THE WISHT HOUNDS

This concerns the burying of suicides and murderers at crossroads, and not on consecrated ground, when, in the case of murderers an oaken stake was also driven through the body to prevent the ghost from haunting the scene. If the stake happened to miss the heart, the ghost was not suppressed, and on the anniversary of the crime, was allowed to assume the mantle of any animal but a sheep, which was then pursued by a savage pack of Wisht hounds and, if he was able to keep more than a coffin's length in front of them, he was free to do the same on the next anniversary. If, however, he was caught, the spell was broken for good and all.

On the anniversary night decent folk, within a mile radius of the spot, stayed indoors, which, in the case in point, meant an area from Dunley around to Little Bovey bridge, up the river to Drake Lane, through the Coombes and around again to Frost Cross at the top of Hatherdown Hill where a murderer was buried. On the night in question, two stout weavers' wives from Bovey, Peggy and Dolly Coniam, had made a midnight start to carry some Dartmoor serge up to Exeter Market.

This was, of course, before the turnpike road was made across Knighton Heath and they were on their way via Frost Cross and Huish to Exeter. They were just climbing over the stile which leads from the church path into Coombe Lane, when they saw the weary hare, (the murderer in animal form), followed by the phosphorescent pack of Wisht hounds coming towards them at a fast pace. Dolly was all for bolting home, but Peggy said: 'No, 'tis no use to rin from the Devil, scripture says us must resist un, we'll stand way back against the haidge an 'old our packs against our stummicks, and Wisht hounds and Devil can't tech us, for they can't abide the zight or zmell of wool. Our saviour was a lamb and his brothers and sisters be sheep, zay your Ave Maria and Paternoster'.

Peggy was right, hare and hounds sped past harmlessly, thanks to the wool and prayers, but the fiend on a black horse was following behind and he scowled as he passed the women. Poor Dolly lost her presence of mind, and from force of good manners dropped a curtsey and said, 'Goodnight Zur', which provoked such a blood curdling yell that both women nearly fainted from fright.

The story did not end with the fright of Dolly and Peggy. It seems a farmer named Tapper, who lived near Newbridge, just in Kingsteignton parish, had agreed a price for a couple of little pigs from farmer Loveys of Hennock, and had gone to fetch them that same evening. He rode a pony, intending to carry the pigs back in a bag across the saddle, so that one hung either side, to balance. The pigs, however, were too young to be weaned, for at least a fortnight, so after a hearty supper he set off for home, his pony knowing the way pretty well.

When they reached Frost Cross however, the pony nearly dislodged his master, for there, sitting up in the road before him was the hare. It did not stir, 'it was runned stiff' said Tapper later, and picking the hare up, put it in his bag, and had just pushed the mouth of the bag between his thigh and the saddle, when the ghostly Wisht hounds tore past on their way up from Coombe. The pony did what Dolly had been going to do, he took fright and bolted home, the bit between his teeth.

In the farmyard, almost dead from fright and excitement, (but by now quite sober), Tapper jumped off his horse, and holding the bag in his hand, took out the hare, which immediately turned into a man, who acquainted him about his past miserable existence, and the legend of the chase, assured him that his crops and stock should from then on be doubled, and promised that the Tapper race should never become extinct from the parish. Nor has it.

THE LEGEND OF THE SARACEN WEDDING GOWN

This concerns a magic wedding dress, and is connected with the stone head, now badly disfigured, which is affixed on the vestry wall in the parish church, over the inner door, said by Ellis to come from a monument he recollects seeing as a boy, in the then north aisle. It showed two men in armour, with their legs crossed, and was known to inhabitants of the town as the Bovey Knights; this head is all that now remains. It seems they were father and son, in this parish. The elder, the father-to-be, went off to join the Crusade of 1291, during the reign of Edward I, and whilst in Nazareth he rescued a wealthy Christian girl, who, in gratitude, gave him her silk damask wedding dress, as a present for the Bovey girl waiting to be his bride on his return.

As happened so many times in those far off days, the wedding did not take place, because on his return, he found she had been married to a man of her father's choice. For some reason, however she persuaded her lover to let her have the gown to keep for her daughter, if she had one.

Later the Crusader married a sister of Bishop Stapledon of Exeter, and sired the son, called Edward. As may be expected in all good legends, Edward fell in love with Alice, the daughter of his father's old love; but she, like her mother, was already betrothed, to a middle aged Squire of Ilsington, and Alice swore she would be a 'Bride of Death' rather than a stepmother to the Squires children.

This vow was unknown to her parents, who allowed her to have a pre-marriage picnic at Haytor, and to this she wore the white damask gown, previously given to her mother. When the picnic was in full swing, and everyone merry-making and drinking, Alice and her maid climbed Haytor Rock, where, planning a suicide attempt, she rushed to the edge of the rock and jumped. But the Saracen gown billowed out like a parachute and carried her safely down to the heather, where Edward was waiting, with a couple of ponies and a marriage licence from the bishop.

They galloped off and were married at Widecombe, while the maid climbed down crying that her mistress had become a 'Bride of Death'. All that remains, for us to verify the legend is the one head still to be seen in the vestry, said by Ellis to be part of the statue, once in the north aisle, and his story, written down from hearsay, but still a good story.

A FURTHER LEGEND OF THE VIRGIN MARY

Although this one is connected with Hyner Farm, in the parish of Hennock, for some reason it has become associated with Bovey legends, and is usually told in conjunction with Bovey history.

It happened one All Hallows Eve, many centuries ago. The miller of Hyner was seated with his wife and young family, around a kitchen table, supping on middlings milk (a mixture of water, milk, and flour middlings); they looked healthy and hearty, and the spoons were moving regularly from bowls to lips. A knock came at the door which the miller opened to find a lady, whose countenance, under her dark hood, was of unearthly sweetness, and she was invited to take a seat at their scanty meal. The miller could not restrain an apology: 'The stream has failed in the long drought, and we cannot gring the grain in the mill, which is why we are supping on middlings'.

The lady hoped he went regularly to church, and the miller replied that at least he sent his family to Mass. She then told them to kneel and say a Paternoster, which they did, and the visitor said that if they continued in their daily devotions, the mill would never again stand idle for want of water.

As she departed, she kissed the unbaptised babe in the cradle, and the little head glowed in the auriole of light. 'Call her Mary, at her baptism', she said, 'In memory of me', and the family realised they had been entertaining the Blessed Virgin. As she went, the rain started to fall in torrents, Hyner brook

rose, and the wheel started to turn again, continuing for many generations, until a heretic miller, who never said a 'Hail Mary', took over and since his day, the brook has failed so often, that now only ruins of the mill can be found on Hyner farm.

BIBLIOGRAPHY AND
SUGGESTED FURTHER READING

Lance Tregoning, *Bovey Tracey in Bygone Days*, Devon Books 1989

Crossing, *Crossings Guide to Dartmoor*, Penninsula Press, 1990

Cecil Torr, *Small Talk in Wreyland*, University Paperbacks, ????date

Ormerods, *Archaeological Memoirs of the East of Dartmoor*, 1876

Brian Adams, *Bovey Tracey Potteries 1750-1836*, B.T. Thorn & Son, 1993

Derek Beavis, *The Templer Way*, Obelisk 1992.

S.C. Jenkins & L.J. Pomroy, *The Moretonhampstead and South Devon Railway*, The Oakwood Press, 1989

Another title by a Bovey author:

Grace Horseman, *Growing Up In The Twenties*, Cottage Publishing 1993.

Available from Cottage Publishing and Bookshop at 72 Fore Street, Bovey Tracey.

INDEX
(SEE ALSO CONTENTS PAGE)